An example of possession and witchcraft which lasted for three years occurred in Illfurth, France. The victims were two young brothers, aged nine and seven. With typical and traditional symptoms of possession, the children whirled about on their backs at fantastic speed, suffered convulsive seizures during which their arms and legs were subject to distorted positions and motions, and on occasion became rigid for hours.

Frequently they yelled obscenities, and apparently were able to speak and understand several languages. Each boy was possessed, presumably, by two devils and, of course, the incredible and fantastic actions and speech were attributed to these evil beings.

It was noted that their seizures became greatly intensified when in the presence of rosaries, holy medals, and the like, and they demonstrated hatred when any mention of the Virgin Mary was made.

The children were finally exorcised and relieved of their fantastic malady. During the course of the exorcism their symptoms became more exaggerated, and one boy had to be confined in a strait jacket on one occasion, so violent were his contortions.

—From *Witchcraft Possession of Two Brothers*

DEDICATION

I dedicate this book to those who made this work possible—all poltergeists past, present and future.

THE
EXORCISM
SERIES
BOOK I
POSSESSED BY THE DEVIL

RAYMOND BAYLESS

(Orig. Title: THE ENIGMA OF THE POLTERGEIST)

ace books
A Division of Charter Communications Inc.
1120 Avenue of the Americas
New York, N.Y. 10036

CONTENTS

Foreword

The best kind of psychical researcher is one who has had personal experiences with unexplainable phenomena. No matter how critical he may be by training, this man believes in the existence of the manifestations, not just theoretically or by hearsay, but actually and empirically. Raymond Bayless is therefore ideally suited to be a researcher in parapsychology because he has had contact with several ghosts and poltergeists. Yet at the same time he is highly critical in his evaluation of each individual experience, even—and most particularly—his own.

Another outstanding attribute which makes Bayless a valuable researcher is his lack of reticence about saying what he has seen, what has convinced him, and what he has rejected as fraud or fantasy. Most writers in this field have a tendency to attempt to be so objective that they feel they are limiting their value as researchers if they express a conviction of any kind, particularly one favorable to the evidence. Actually, a new era of writing is now under way in parapsychology. Previous books have been either too restrained, because their authors have felt reluctant to be considered naïve, or else so overwhelmingly uncritical that their writers *were* obviously naïve. Fortunately, some recent writers have begun to be more free in their statements. If they have seen psychical phenomena under controlled conditions which to them were conclusive, they have admitted it; and yet they have retained their ability to evaluate critically what they saw and what others have purported to have seen. Raymond Bayless is one of those.

This author's personal quality makes him an exceptionally able researcher in an area which demands non-conformity of the most determined sort. Characteristically, he became proficient in a difficult task by his own efforts. His success as a professional artist is a perfect illustration of this. When Raymond Bayless was young he became impressed and obsessed with the beauty and technique of the classic Dutch school of art. In an era in which Abstract Expressionism was considered to be the only thing of importance in painting, no one was even teaching these Dutch techniques of delicate meticulous detail of representation and high gloss finishes. And so Raymond Bayless, who wished to paint the naturalistic and realistic way instead of the abstract, had to learn for himself. He acquired all of his techniques entirely by his own effort. His art is completely self-taught, and yet he has achieved the top of his profession. Although he has shown in most of the better galleries on the West Coast, his beautiful paintings are so eagerly sought that they are purchased almost before they are completed, and he finds it difficult to get enough of them together to hold a show.

Until the past year he has featured still life painting, all done with tiny brushes in the most exquisite detail. At present, however, he has become enamoured of landscapes and is concentrating on them exclusively; but, even here he does nothing which could be considered in any possible way modern. His new paintings remind one of early American landscapes, and this is for a special reason: he has taught himself to paint in the tradition of the Hudson River school, which is known as a continuation of the Dutch school.

The same endless patience, practice, and constant experimentation which Raymond Bayless has used to achieve success as an artist, he also has used in his avocation—psychical research. He has familiarized himself with a vast amount of the literature of the field, and has followed up every clue in every case which

8

has come to his attention. This book, while giving a resume of the historical poltergeist, is also interspersed with a few of its author's personal experiences, as he made it a point for a number of years to investigate personally as many cases as possible which have occurred in California. He also tries to determine an explanation for the poltergeist. It must be admitted that here he, like most of his contemporaries, has been forced to arrive at the conclusion that there are a number of nebulous explanations, all of them difficult to comprehend or evaluate.

In this modern world it is easy to delude ourselves into thinking that science knows all the answers to the actual realities of life, and that anything unexplainable must therefore be an hallucination or else untrue to the facts in some other way. Yet every new achievement by physicists, chemists and astronomers takes us just a little bit closer to the realization that we are still far from knowing the ultimate basis of reality. With all their talk about the conscious and the unconscious, psychologists readily admit that they don't really know what the Mind is. As C. P. Snow says, "The further scientists analyze, the less obvious the answers become."

When physicists and chemists finally turn their attention to the poltergeist, which will be extremely difficult to study in a laboratory because no repeatable experiments can be devised, perhaps we can find an answer to this amazing curiosity which has occurred throughout the ages. Until then we can only be grateful to men like Raymond Bayless who give their time and effort to what can only be considered a thankless task. The fact that the poltergeist is also a challenge of the utmost fascination is the thing that keeps men like him so entranced with it.

Susy Smith

Author's Introduction

Psychical research, or parapsychology, is one of the most important fields of investigation within the body of science, and, in fact, may be the most important field in all scientific endeavor. Included in the many branches of psychical research are phenomena of the most intriguing nature, and certainly one of the most baffling, bizarre, mysteries is that of the poltergeist.

The reality of the ghostly force is still considered controversial; but, to many of those engaged in parapsychological studies, it is thoroughly documented, and its existence is beyond dispute. Numerous scientists of world renown have not only admitted that evidence for the existence of such phenomena is overwhelming in quantity, but have themselves witnessed the grotesque actions of the poltergeist. Names of great scientific fame such as Prof. Cesare Lombroso, Prof. James Hyslop, Sir William Barrett, Prof. Hans Thirring, Dr. R. J. Tilyard and Prof. William McDougall can be included in this list.

The poltergeist includes within its spectrum of activities a wide choice of effects. One of the most commonly found manifestations is the mysterious stone-throwing that frequently finds mention in the press. Cases of this nature may last from a few days to many months. The missiles may arrive at high speeds or may descend in abnormally slow fall. To compound this mystery the rocks may be unusually warm or cold.

Another well-known effect of the poltergeist (so much so as to be practically a matter of folklore) is the sound of raps. Ghostly rappings range from the lightest of taps to loud powerful blows.

Fantastic fires of unearthly origin have been frequently encountered. One blaze after another may spring up within a house with no apparent cause, and during one extreme infestation a home was completely destroyed.

Strange influxes of water have been recorded and provide a rare characteristic of the poltergeist. Water and other liquids have appeared within buildings in quantities varying from slight sprinkles to fantastic flows.

Smashed dishes and thrown pots and pans have performed aerial acrobatics to such an extent that the mysterious force has earned the title of kitchen ghost. Mysterious movements of objects, both mild and violent, are not confined to the kitchen, however, for furniture of every kind and objects of all descriptions have danced to the whim of the poltergeist.

Rare effects are those of voices and apparitions. Voices have been reported which spoke, yelled, whispered, and in short, duplicated human utterance in every way. Apparitions have been seen, but usually are found in rare, complex haunting.

These are but a few of the many manifestations of the poltergeist, and it can be seen that this baffling force at times reminds one of a Boschian phantasmagoria.

Many of the complex, famous cases which offer descriptions of exotic phenomena have occurred many years in the past, and it has been suggested that these accounts are greatly exaggerated. This is possible although the reports seem to have been the product of careful and thorough consideration. Again it must be remembered that the diversity and violence of such examples can be matched by cases of more recent years.

From a researcher's point of view I have had the good fortune to have personally witnessed poltergeist/ haunting manifestations and examples of major phenomena during experimental seances. Resultingly, I find it not too difficult to accept well-documented, complex cases that have been reported. Certain of my personal experiences are given in this book.

The nature of the poltergeist is only partially understood, but the solution is based on mystery—the mystery of paranormal phenomena. Apparently, the eerie force is born in the unconscious and can be a result of tensions, unresolved conflicts, resentments and frustrations. On occasion, the powers released may have curative effects. The intelligence displayed may vary from apparently blind, mechanical reactions to activities seemingly equal to that of a normal person.

Maliciousness is characteristic of the majority of cases, though many manifestations superficially appear to be quite aimless. In this respect the poltergeist is a force not to be feared. Only in the very complex cases can actual viciousness and physical danger be considered a tangible possibility, and such cases are very rare indeed! Psychological dangers, however, must be considered. The intelligence, or directive force, so frequently found with the poltergeist poses a problem admitting no easy solution. I believe that a large percentage of the phenomena observed originates from within the subconscious mind of the inadvertent "poltergeist medium" and represents one facet of the mind temporarily acting in an apparently independent fashion. I also believe that in certain cases intervention of the dead does occur.

Knowledge of the poltergeist is, I believe, a very valuable acquisition. It can enable one to be of help to those troubled by these baffling disturbances, dispel needless fears, and offer beneficial suggestive therapy.

The last and perhaps most valuable gift that such knowledge bestows is a re-affirmation of the sense of grandeur and wonder brought about by our awareness of the great mysteries of our universe.

chapter 1

The Mysterious Activities of the Poltergeist

Manifestations Greatly Varied

In all the varied and fascinating forms manifested by psychical phenomena, perhaps the most exotic effects are those found with the poltergeist and hauntings. Arthur Machen's comments in his *London Adventure* well express the sense of the wondrous, and the grotesque, that envelop such activity when he commented upon a poltergeist case that he investigated. Machen remarked upon the fact that the sum total of things of which we are aware is incredibly strange, and that at the heart of the world are infinite beauties and unbelievable curiosities.

It can be safely said that with the poltergeist, every form of psychical phenomena both in the experimental seance and in spontaneous cases, has been reported, and the sheer diversity of manifestation is truly incredible. It is almost impossible to list all the strange, individual actions attributed to the poltergeist, and so I shall briefly mention a number of the main categories of phenomena that have been encountered, and in the following chapters describe various types of individual cases which will, I am sure, provide an overall picture of the poltergeist's effects.

Defining the Poltergeist

Defining the poltergeist, and hauntings, is difficult. They, or it, can be expressed as a mysterious force which can lodge itself everywhere. It may infest a home, a shop, a church and soon make itself known by any single phenomenon which will be described, or by any combination of such. Both poltergeists and hauntings can be said to be a force, a disembodied energy, capable of creating the various manifestations to be described. The origin of this force is still another profound problem offering several possible solutions as discussed in this book.

Though the subject of this work is the poltergeist proper, the phenomena of hauntings must be constantly mentioned as they are inextricably interwoven with the poltergeist. It is impossible to refer to one without mentioning the other.

Fall of Stones a Common Effect

Probably, the first effect to come to mind is the mysterious showers of stones that so frequently occur, and we find these odd happenings periodically mentioned in the press. Numerous examples of rock-throwings have existed unaccompanied by other phenomena, and yet, paranormal stone-throwings can be found in cases yielding all types of paranormal activity.

The history of these mysterious showers of stones is of great antiquity. Hereward Carrington, for example, compiled a list of poltergeist cases, many including stone-falls, reaching back hundreds of years.

The very first case listed offering thrown stones took place in 335 A.D. When various cases of all periods are compared, a remarkable similarity becomes evident. The peculiar slow fall of the stones, the strange paths of flight, the temperature oddities, and the like, are all familiar stigmata, and have been the subject of wonder throughout the centuries.

Mysterious Fires Occur

Fires of mysterious origin, some harmless and others violently destructive, are typical poltergeist manifestations, and in fact, certain grim phenomena associated with spontaneous human combustion may possibly be laid at the poltergeist's door.

Here we have an apparent contradiction of a favorite belief which assumes that poltergeist phenomena is harmless, and seldom, if ever, resulting in serious injury and really is rather amusing after all. This cheerful view soon assumes somber tones when the actual histories of many cases are reviewed, and a very formidable figure indeed comes to view. There is a considerable body of evidence which clearly indicates that the poltergeist can be a savage and fearful enemy, possessing grim and mysterious powers.

Not only have people been killed by fantastic fires, but they have also died as a result of strange attacks by all types of missiles. For further study in this area the works of Charles Fort should be consulted. At the very least, considering the evidence at hand, a strong case exists indicating an extremely dangerous side to the poltergeist.

Of course, the well-known telekinetic flights of all types of objects are a matter, practically, of folk lore. Dishes are a special target and pots and pans are traditional aerial acrobats. Even heavy furniture has been mysteriously moved about, and all objects pertaining to the home have been subject to the whim of the poltergeist.

Mysterious Odors Reported

Strange odors are frequently encountered, which unaccountably vanish as mysteriously as they arise. Some scents are sweet and would seem to be the pure fragrance of flowers, yet others can be repulsive and disgusting. They may come in an instant, filling a room so completely as to seem near stifling, and just as instantaneously leave.

Unusual Sounds Are Heard

Poltergeists are prone to producing sounds of all descriptions; whispers, whistles, sobs, groans, the sounds of moving clothing, crashes, explosive noises—and speech! A curious feature of these sounds is the fact that they may seem as though the house is being broken up, piece by piece, and still, upon investigation, nothing has been disturbed. Of course, many sounds are actually caused by objects being knocked about and are of earthly, physical origin.

Rappings and Poundings Typical

Rappings, poundings, and scratchings are common effects of the poltergeist. The rappings can range from light tappings and creaks to violent blows that literally shake the house. During many cases, the rappings have answered questions, showing intelligence, but on the other hand, cases exist where houses have been subject to mysterious poundings and rappings which were apparently aimless in nature.

Apparitions Are Seen

Apparitions have appeared in poltergeist-infested, or haunted houses, and have, at times, presented the traditional, classic ghost. Noiseless, shadowy figures have appeared and disappeared mysteriously, some dressed in antique style, and others in quite modern dress. Phantoms have shown on occasion a definite awareness of their startled onlookers, and others have glided about their ghostly way betraying no interest in their involuntary audiences.

Ghostly Voices Have Been Heard

Speaking ghosts and poltergeists have been reported many times. Ghostly voices have occurred with other types of phenomena; some examples displayed awareness of surrounding circumstances, and entered into conversation with the surprised occupants of the haunted house, and others have merely spoken in fragmentary sentences indicating no knowledge of the onlookers. These voices usually occur as disembodied sounds, but occasionally are heard in the presence of a visible phantom.

The Saragossa Ghost, a case which acquired great attention in 1934, offered the purest example of this particular phenomenon, and did nothing but talk. No other phenomena was noted; no visible apparitions were seen, and nothing else took place beyond a remarkable voice which emanated from a chimney. It was very aware of its audience and was obviously connected with a 16 year-old servant girl.

Objects Appear and Disappear

Objects appear and disappear in a most bewildering fashion. Keys are taken from locks, clothes are discovered missing when wanted, and, in general, the behavior of the poltergeist can be annoying and malicious.

The inventiveness of the poltergeist to produce phenomena is only limited by the number of objects available, and so, it is not really possible to list all the feats accomplished by the infesting force. If a chair is handy, it may be moved across the room. If a dish is on a table, it will soon be thrown and broken. And to add further to an already enormous list of possible actions, phenomena can occur which apparently are not based in the physical world. Mysterious crashing sounds may be heard, but upon search, they cannot be correlated to any broken object. Voices may speak, yet are unrelated to any person present, and so the poltergeist not only has all the endless possibilities of the physical world at its disposal, but those of an immaterial world as well.

Hauntings and Poltergeists Closely Related

To differentiate clearly between a case of haunting and one of poltergeist activity is difficult, if not really impossible. Both contain elements common to each other and partake of much the same phenomena. A "haunted house," for instance, is generally pictured with a "ghost" and accompanying strange sounds, but again, the poltergeist-infested house behaves in much the same way. Perhaps the one characteristic that seems to be different is that poltergeist phenomena does seem, in general, to be annoying and malicious, and at times, dangerous and destructively malignant. The haunted house is not usually viewed in this manner. However, what is to prevent one from asking, "Why cannot the poltergeist on occasion merely be a 'haunt' with a foul disposition?"

To further complicate the problem, spontaneous phenomena, effects encountered in the experimental seance, poltergeist phenomena and hauntings—all bear a remarkable resemblance to each other. The experimental seance may yield rappings, phantasmal figures, telekinetic movement of objects, and a whole host of happenings, all of which have occurred in poltergeist cases.

Spirit Origin Elementary View

Probably none but the most naive Spiritualist believes today that the poltergeist is necessarily an actual human spirit. I have heard just this view expressed and included in a newspaper article describing a rock-fall case in Big Bear City in California as follows: "There are souls that have left this earth-plane. They have learned on the other side how to materialize energy and cause dishes or furniture to move." These remarks represent the primitive views of the early Spiritualists, for they also assumed an actual human spirit running about, causing and directing any and all phenomena that was observed in either the seance room, or during spontaneous happenings.

It would be difficult to imagine a ghost, a spirit, running about, throwing each rock during falls. It would require undoubtedly a full baseball team to accomplish such a remarkable feat. Another view exists which suggests that a "nature spirit," or "elemental" is responsible for the phenomena, but again it is still the same mechanism with a new title.

It is quite true that not only have stones been thrown in poltergeist cases, but all types of objects have been hurled. During the incredible happenings that took place in the Ringcroft case in 1695, a very remarkable list of thrown objects can be compiled. Stones of all sizes were chosen missiles, of course, and lumps of burning peat, staves, a plowshare, bundles of burning straw, "fireballs," spades, mud, etc, were all thrown by the versatile poltergeist.

This case is not an isolated example, for during the poltergeist outbreak known as the Stockwell Ghost in 1772, an equally diverse list of projectiles was compiled. Eggs were thrown, as well as dishes and glasses, a mortar and pestle, a teapot, and a candlestick.

Poltergeist Cases Increasing

At times it has been asked if poltergeist cases are not diminishing in number, and of course, the inference is that with a more scientific attitude and correspondingly more rigid and demanding investigations, the number of cases is drastically reduced. It has been then suggested that this argument be carried out to its logical end, and with a completely controlled and foolproof investigation there will be no case that can stand the cold light of scientific inquiry.

As a matter of fact, the sheer number of poltergeist cases and related phenomena is most definitely on the increase. Article after article appears in the newspapers and magazines, and cases are frequently discussed on television and the radio. There are two reasons for this increase of cases reported, and one is the very obvious fact that reluctance to mention such a controversial subject is diminishing. To admit that poltergeist phenomena do exist is no longer considered an admission of mental and moral degeneracy and a social stigma is no longer the invariable result of such belief. As a consequence of increasing public information and scientific studies, newspapers are not fearful to furnish their readers with accounts of these mysteries.

Most articles are timid and faltering in their approach, and at times antagonistic to the very concept of such a paranormal force as the poltergeist and hauntings. Still, accounts do appear in print. I am hopeful that, with the further passage of time, we will be treated to far more articles of this nature, and the reporting will become less timid and eventually will be factual and relatively unbiased.

The other reason for the increase in numbers of cases encountered is due to the simple fact that populations over the world are drastically increasing. With the enormous rise in sheer numbers of human beings, there must, of necessity, be an equally large increase in poltergeist cases. Of course, it is impossible to ever obtain a truly comprehensive and accurate list of such cases, but if such were possible, there no doubt would be a direct relationship between population and the number of cases.

Subject's Educational Level Unrelated to Phenomena

It has been a more or less accepted belief that with the increase of knowledge and general education, and a corresponding change of beliefs and attitudes, psychical phenomena tends to decrease. With such changes, the individual susceptability to paranormal happenings lessens. However, I do not believe this is at all true, for poltergeist phenomena occur under all circumstances. The individuals who are favored or cursed, according to their opinion, are of all degrees of education and social standing. An outbreak may take place in the home of the extremely poor, and bears no relationship apparently to the degree of information and sophistication that one may possess.

CHAPTER HIGHLIGHTS

The poltergeist is varied in its actions. It has duplicated every phenomenon observed in the experimental seance. Some typical effects are falls of stones, fires, odors, movement of objects, voices, rappings, poundings, apparitions, etc. The popular belief of spirit origin is not adequate. The number of cases is increasing. The poltergeist is unrelated to educational levels and social standing.

chapter   2

The Poltergeist Throughout the Ages

A Brief List of Cases

The story of the poltergeist is as old as history. There are accounts of ghostly disturbances from ancient Egypt, from Greece and Rome, and the lives of the Christian mystics and Saints furnish many early examples. Certainly, one of the first recorded cases involving paranormal stone-throwing occurred in 355 A.D., and, in fact, Hereward Carrington began his well-known list of historic poltergeist cases here.

It has been remarked that religion began with the belief in, and the fear of, ghosts, and that the idea of ghosts originated in dreams of departed relatives, parents, and so on. Not only is the first part of this observation an entirely unwarranted assumption, but the second half can also stand considerable correction. It is far better to say that the belief in ghosts began with ghosts! Undoubtedly, primitive man encountered ghostly phenomena and suffered visitations of the poltergeist, and as a result found himself believing in such beings.

The list of noted historical poltergeist cases has been the subject of several works devoted to the field, and to repeat it is unnecessary. However, a number of the very famous examples must be mentioned for the sake of historical continuity. Other examples not so well-known will also be described as well as recent cases that have not been published.

No history can possibly be written of the poltergeist without referring to the famous and classical Drummer of Tedworth. There are, naturally, many earlier cases, but a start must be made somewhere. The Rev. Joseph Glanvil first published his account of this fascinating disturbance in his *"Philosophical Considerations concerning the existence of Sorcerers and Sorcery"* in 1666. Numerous other accounts soon followed. To summarize very briefly, Mr. John Mompesson of Tedworth discovered, after a bit of legal complexity with an itinerant drummer, that his home had become the scene of near incredible poltergeist phenomena of a definitely malignant cast. Interestingly, the drummer while at trial claimed that he was responsible for the disturbance, and in making this somewhat sensational claim was rather foolhardy, inasmuch as execution for witchcraft was still practiced; the last execution in England for this offense occurred in 1682.

Practically the entire gamut of poltergeist and haunting effects were encountered. Knockings and poundings of all degrees were heard. Sulfurous odors were created. All types of objects were thrown about. Lights were seen and a mysterious voice was heard.

The poltergeist, as we have mentioned, manifested extreme ferocity and displayed the almost traditional maliciousness, and at times, positive fury, when confronted by actions or objects of a devotional nature.

A Bible was found in the ashes and it was noticed that the open side was placed downward and that it lay open at the third chapter of St. Mark where reference is made to unclean spirits falling down before Christ and to His giving power to cast out devils. This interesting and significant action revealed a definite intelligence in that an appropriate passage had been chosen which aptly applied to the invading poltergeist. Its ill will to the sentiment expressed is indicated by the placement of the open page in the ashes. Here, we have a typical example of the poltergeist's dislike of things of a religious nature.

The phenomena finally ceased and quiet came at last to the house besieged by a mysterious and fantastic force. Rev. Glanvil's final comments are interesting and are appropriate to any thorough investigation today.

I had thus related the sum of the story, and noted some circumstances that assure the truth of it. I confess the passages recited are not so dreadful, tragical and amazing, as there are some in a story of this kind, yet they are nevertheless probable or true, for their being not so prodigious and astonishing. And they are strange enough to prove themselves effects of some invisible extraordinary agent, and so demonstrate in our affairs. And I think they do it with clearness of evidence. For these things were not done long ago, or at a far distance, in an ignorant age, or among a barbarous people, they were not seen by two or three only of the melancholic and superstitious, and reported by those that made them serve the advantage and interest of a party. They were not passages of a Day or Night, nor the vanishing glances of an Apparition; but these transactions were near and late, public, frequent, and divers years continuance, witnessed by multitudes of competent and unbiased attestors, and acted in a searching incredulous age: arguments enough one would think to convince any modern and capable reason.[1]

Across the Atlantic in New England parallel phenomena were occurring and added fury to the flames of the witchcraft fires that were beginning to burn. Increase Mather chronicled a series of mysterious happenings that we now can safely assume were attributable to poltergeists. Naturally, this coincidence of real phenomena and the pseudo-phenomena of the witchcraft epidemic was unfortunate in the extreme and could hardly have failed to inflame already overheated imaginations.

In 1679 the home of William Morse in Newberry, New England, was besieged by a bombardment of blows upon the roof and several days later five stones and bricks were thrown in the house, the bedstead was lifted up from the floor, and a cat was thrown at his wife. Further incidents followed and no household article was safe from the poltergeist.

The family was continually struck by various objects and some of these blows, to judge by the description, must have been severe and painful. A passage by Mather well illustrates this point:

[1]Harry Price, *Poltergeist Over England*, Country Life Ltd., 1945. Quotations from the Ringcroft, Tedworth and Hinton Ampner Cases, his chapter heading, "Can we explain The Poltergeist?," "No. Cannot Be Exorcised—With Exceptions," are from the same source.

The night following, they went to bed undressed, because of their late disturbances, and the man, wife, boy, presently felt themselves pricked and upon search found in the bed a bodkin, a knitting needle, and two sticks picked at both ends; he received also a great blow, as on his thigh, so on his face, which fetched blood; and while he was writing, a candlestick was twice thrown at him; and a great piece of bark fiercely smote him; and a pail of water turned up without hands.

Ultimately, the phenomena centered upon the boy. He was, according to report, struck by all manner of missiles, and subject to a fantastic and grotesque persecution until at last he "barked like a dog, and clucked like a hen; and after long distraining to speak, said, 'There's Powel, I am pinched.' His tongue likewise hung out of his mouth, so that it could by no means be forced in till his fit was over. . . ."

Further grotesque symptoms were betrayed by the boy and his afflictions became more complex. Mather wrote: "The boy was growing antick as he was on the journey, but before the end of it he made a grievous hollowing; and when he lighted, he threw a great stone at a maid in the house, and fell on eating ashes. Being at home afterwards, they had to rest awhile: but on the 19th of January, in the morning he swooned, and coming to himself, he roared terribly, and did eat ashes, sticks, rug-yarn."

One can imagine the fearful state of mind of the boy and his family, for dwelling upon the dark, terrible stories of witches and their dreaded powers. With their thoughts already beset by terror, they must have surely thought the forces of evil were upon them. Fear, of course, brought hysterical mimicry, and the actions of those who had presumably undergone persecution by witchcraft were inevitably imitated, and compounding these terrors were the visible and tangible phenomena of the poltergeist.

New Manifestations Added

As the persecution continued new manifestations were added and on one occasion a scraping on boards occurred, followed by a piping and drumming, and an audible voice singing. "Revenge, Sweet is revenge." The terrified family called upon heaven for aid, and the voice was reported to have replied, "Alas, me knock no more, me knock no more," and all was quiet.

Curiously, a visiting seaman insisted that the boy's mother, suspected of witchcraft, was innocent and was wrongly accused, and that the boy was actually at the bottom of the infestation. Stating that the house would be troubled no more if he could have the boy for one day, the seaman took him with him and, "Since which time his house, he saith has not been molested with spirits."

This discernment of the visitor was remarkable and one wonders how complete his understanding was of the fact that the curious happenings emanated from the afflicted boy rather than being a product of witchcraft. The remarks of the seaman have a most modern ring and it is really unfortunate that there is no way of knowing just how closely his thoughts paralleled the present psychological theories. Possibly the story of the voice exultingly exclaiming the sweetness of revenge furnished a clue. Certainly, the seaman's words suggest that he had considerably more insight into the mysterious and frightening happenings than his contemporaries. We are left with a minor, but intriguing mystery.

Mather described further instances of apparent poltergeist phenomena in New England and wrote about Nicholas Desbrough, who had been beset by thrown stones, clods, corncobs, and other missiles. The manifestations seemed to have been triggered by a quarrel about a chest of clothes which Desbrough kept, although it apparently did not belong to him. He was eventually ordered to return the chest of clothes and the disturbances ceased.

Another interesting example was recorded by Mather which began June 11th, 1682, and again involved falling stones and other objects. Other phenomena were also reported. It was claimed by some members of the family afflicted that a hand unattached to a body was seen throwing stones. We will encounter this ghostly hand again and again, as it is one of the prominent, visible manifestations of the poltergeists. A hollow whistling was also heard as well as other strange sounds.

There have been strange and true reports concerning a woman now living near Salman Falls Barwick (formerly called Kittery), unto whom evil spirits have sometimes visibly appeared; and she has sometimes been sorely tempted by invisible hands; concerning all which an intelligent person has sent me the following narrative.

Thus Mather introduces a last case which seems to be mixed with the pseudo-phenomena of witchcraft. It undoubtedly is of much less authenticity than the foregoing examples, in that the incidents reported which ring true for genuine poltergeist effects are diluted by observations resulting from the prevailing acceptance of sorcery.

In June, 1682, a voice was heard by the wife of Antonio Hertado at the door of her home which said, "What do you do here?" About an hour after she was struck over the eye and several days from then, a stone was thrown, and a frying pan struck. The couple left their house and claimed that while crossing a river in a boat, they saw the head of a man and the white tail of a cat close together swimming nearby. Upon returning they again claimed they saw this fantastic being. Further attacks upon the woman occurred including another thrown stone, scratchings, and bites upon her arm. The impressions of the teeth were plainly visible according to the account.

Here we have one of the more exotic phenomena in the biting and scratching, and, of course, the case of Eleanore Zugun immediately comes to mind. As is well-known, this poltergeist-victim, widely studied by noted and reputable scientists, frequently displayed bites and scratches. She also possessed remarkable telekinetic abilities that were observed under excellent conditions.

Father Herbert Thurson, S. J., includes in his collections of cases, an example of a biting poltergeist and the case is entitled, *"An Account of Disturbance, etc., at the Lamb, Without Lawford's Gate,"* which occurred during the years 1761 and 1762.

To return to our New England haunting, Hertado's wife, Mary, insisted that a woman appeared to her and attempted to strike her with a burning brand. The following day the same apparition appeared again and Mary suffered no further difficulties.

Her husband, however, heard footsteps in his room and a few other manifestations were said to have taken place. His wife had been advised to place certain protective plants about the house and when they finally lost their green color they were mysteriously removed and she was again troubled.

Naturally, at this far distant date it is impossible to arrive at any definite conclusion, but it is possible that certain genuine poltergeist phenomena had taken place, and that the real effects were embellished with stories borrowed from prevailing witchcraft lore. The grotesque, composite figure "seen" swimming in the river, and the apparition of the threatening female figure were plainly derived from traditional sorcery, and there seems little reason to believe other than that the phantom woman was merely an interpolated witch.

A remarkable and famous outbreak occurred in 1695 which presented an amazing collection of paranormal effects including the ever-present thrown stones. This case, the Ringcroft Poltergeist, included numerous fires in the course of one day. People were pulled about and struck by sticks, prayers were interrupted, intelligible voices were heard on several occasions; "fireballs" fell in the house, whistles and groans sounded, and a small, white hand and arm "from the elbow down" appeared.

The appearance of the hand and arm is extremely interesting, and, as we have noticed, played an important part in many cases. It casts a light upon the problem of the poltergeist-force itself and also upon the problem of whether or not the poltergeist is ever visible. This significant phenomenon will be discussed later.

As in the Tedworth infestation and the well-known persecutions of many Christian mystics, abhorrence was displayed whenever prayers were offered, and, in fact, the efforts of five ministers to exorcise the fearful visitor were fruitless. For example, stones were thrown at any engaged in prayers.

Case after case followed. The very well-known haunting of the family of John Wesley which took place during December and January, 1716-1717, has been described many times, and so we will only mention that it was a comparatively simple case, consisting primarily of knockings. However, a few other phenomena were recorded including the "appearance" of a ghostly figure that came down a staircase, groans, and a sound like "the quick winding-up of a jack," and a small animal apparition was seen three times. The animal form was described as appearing as a white rabbit, and at another time, "most like a badger."

Do Poltergeists Show Intelligence?

At this point, it seems appropriate to recall that some writers have remarked that the poltergeist always displays a sameness in phenomena and little or no imagination is used. Reviewing the many cases over the years, I fail to convince myself that this observation is correct. In view of events that have been described, and the amazing and varied manifestations that have taken place, I would say that the poltergeist is instead gifted with an extremely fertile imagination, and is quick to seize upon any possibility of action limited only by the number of available objects handy, possibly has at times a sense of humor, and in general possesses a splendid power of invention.

To be more exact, the poltergeist is not really limited to material objects available, for many effects seem to be drawn from a non-physical world. In fact, if a normal human were granted the power of invisibility and directed to plague a home by any means possible, short of actual murder—and I retain very definite reservations regarding this possibility—it would be hard indeed to match the versatility of the poltergeist. One could throw household objects such as dishes, glasses, chairs, and what have you, smashing a good number in the process, and, for variety, toss stones at the house both inside and out. Threatening gestures could be made with the stones, or any handy object, occasionally striking the nearest target, either human or otherwise, but in the case of the human target not with full force so as to avoid injuring them. A further nasty activity could be accomplished by hiding desired objects and this could prove gloriously infuriating.

If one felt a bit more destructive fires could be started, though being reasonably sure that they would be found before going completely out of control. Scaring people could be nicely done by pounding the walls, doors, etc., and eerie footsteps would have a splendid shocking effect. Threatening statements spoken aloud, or written, and choice fantastic remarks would be of the greatest aid, and within a reasonable time a household could be reduced to a very rewarding state of terror and collapse.

If our theoretical, invisible human was actually bent upon serious evil and had little compunction regarding life itself, then major injury could well be inflicted, or murder itself could be easily accomplished. The possibility for destructive persecution would be almost unlimited.

To return to the Wesley haunting—among the correspondence communicated by Rev. S. Babcock, edited in 1791 by Joseph Priestly, we discover a little-known "Memorandum of Jack's," which states that: "The first time my mother ever heard an unusual noise at Epworth was long before the disturbances of old Jeffry. (The family name for the poltergeist.) My brother, lately come from London, had in the evening a sharp quarrel with my sister Sukey." Knockings followed and, "doors and windows rung and jarred," and these oddities occurred during all times of family excitement and before death. Therefore, we see that the haunting at Epworth Parsonage was well established before the traditional date for the onslaught of the poltergeist.

Particularly Complex Cases

Other famous cases occurred about the same period as did the Ringcroft Poltergeist and the Drummer of Tedworth and some of these cases were extremely complex and presented a large variety of phenomena. An interesting case entitled "The Burton Poltergeist" took place in Somerset and the evidence was taken down in 1677. Phenomena on the order of that observed during the Ringcroft disturbance, though not so complex in nature, occurred.

The Hinton Ampner haunting is another of the famous historical cases. The first recorded phenomenon at the manor occurred soon after the death of Lord Stawell in 1765 when a groom claimed to have seen the phantom of the dead man. Later, the house was let to the Ricketts who endured a seige of frightening incidents from 1765 to 1771. Phantoms were seen, including a "woman dressed in dark clothes which rustled as though a very stiff silk," ghostly walking noises, knockings, shrieks and mysterious voices were heard. The house was finally destroyed after another family rented it in 1772, experienced phantasmic phenomena, and left in 1773.

In the year 1762, the noted, or as some would prefer it, the infamous Cock Lane Ghost mystery took place, and as is quite well-known, many consider that it was a complete fraud from the beginning. Various scratching and rappings were heard and a simple code was soon established, and communication achieved with the "ghostly" rapper. Dr. Johnson was present at one of the seances and afterwards wrote an account discounting the entire affair. In a chapter devoted to the Cock Lane Ghost, Harry Price, in his *Poltergeist Over England* remarked that in his opinion there were some genuine effects observed.

Across the Atlantic the poltergeist was still quite busy. A very interesting case occurred in 1797 in a home in the village of Middleway, West Virginia. The haunting was described in a rather obscure book by Rev. Peter H. Lemcke, entitled *The Life and Work of Prince Demetrius Agustine Gallitizin.* The usual bag of tricks of the poltergeist was displayed, objects were hurled about in daylight and "ungodly noises" were heard at night. Articles of clothing hanging on the walls and locked in chests were cut to ribbons and provisions stored in the pantry were found mixed together and subsequently ruined.

Apparitions were said to have commonly occurred and a girl who was obviously the unwitting, inadvertant medium, suffered so from the unwelcome attentions of the poltergeist that she was believed near death at one time.

Attempts were made by Methodist ministers to restore peace to the beleaguered house, but to no avail. The greater their efforts, the more violent became the poltergeist. A pillow was thrown into the face of one witness while singing hymns and another had a bowl of sour milk dumped on top of his head.

Finally, the owners of the disturbed house, after preparing to abandon it completely, allowed a priest, Rev. Dennis Cahill, to attempt exorcism. His efforts brought peace to the infested house. Prince Gallitizin, a priest, made an investigation of the haunting and wrote a report detailing the disturbance, but unfortunately the original report was lost.

An example of haunting that consisted entirely of the paranormal ringing of bells used to summon servants occurred at Great Bealing in East Suffolk, and lasted from February 2 to March 27, 1834. The case was published by Major Edward Moore, Fellow of the Royal Society, in 1841, along with a number of other similar cases.

Another very well known disturbance, "The Haunted House at Willington," began its paranormal history in 1835 and lasted for many years. The phenomena recorded were very complex and yielded footsteps, knockings, noises of furniture being moved about, bell ringing, many apparitions, including a small monkey, or monkey-like phantom, and numerous other eerie and fantastic effects.

It might be added as a matter of interest that the French dramatist, Victorien Sardou remarked that he had at one time been definitely mediumistic, experiencing many paranormal incidents and stated that his guiding spirits at last left him while he was writing. Sardou said: "I had been writing when suddenly my pen was split into matchwood in my hand. . . ." In this incident we have a phenomenon very reminiscent of the poltergeist.

A case that caused great controversy in the press in 1897 was the noted Ballechin House haunting. Certainly one of its claims to fame was the researchers involved in its study. Miss A. Goodrich-Freer, Mr. F. W. H. Myers, and Sir Oliver Lodge were all engaged in the study of the house and its phenomena. Thumpings, knocks, footsteps, groans, and the very unpleasant trick of pulling the bedclothes away were all part of the poltergeist's manifestation. Voices and a shriek were also heard on occasion. Sir Oliver Lodge stated that he had heard knocks, droning and wailing sounds, and remarked that he had found the phenomena interesting and considered that some of the raps definitely indicated intelligence. Miss Goodrich-Freer published a famous account of the case with Lord Bute, which bore the title, *The Alleged Haunting of B . . . . . House,* and a description of the haunting can be found in Harry Price's *Poltergeist Over England.*

Numerous cases of immense interest and value can be found described in Professor Camille Flammarion's splendid work, *Haunted Houses.* Among the more outstanding cases are the troubled house of Las Constantine and the incredible haunting of Calvados Castle. These cases are a must for the student of poltergeist phenomena. Probably the last has never been surpassed for sheer violence and horrific effects.

We have, of course, the classic haunting entitled *The Great Amherst Mystery* which was described by Walter Hubbell and was published in New York in 1888. The case occurred in Nova Scotia in the village of Amherst and revolved around the poltergeist-medium, Esther Cox. Active and varied manifestations were observed; and accounts of the disturbance can be found in various modern books including Sacheverell Sitwell's *Poltergeists, Fact or Fancy.* The case is disputed by various authorities, but Hereward Carrington, for example, considered that genuine phenomena were encountered.

This annoying mixture of fraud and real phenomena is a traditional hazard faced by the psychical researcher, and the investigation of poltergeist cases presents the same difficulty. It is a recognized fact that a perfectly genuine poltergeist-medium may suddenly succumb to the urge to augment the real effects by fraud. The Lynwood rock-throwing poltergeist case presented a classical example and will be described fully in a later chapter. Needless to say, this can complicate the situation quite a bit, but the investigator must take it all in his stride.

The occasional mixture of fraud and phenomena can prove to be an insurmountable hurdle to the amateur investigator who finds, at times, that all is not black and white, but sometimes gray.

A remarkable poltergeist case centered around a young Rumanian girl, Eleanore Zugun, who was born in 1913. Many extraordinary effects were observed in her presence, including objects that burst, such as an iron pot, and a stone was thrown at a picture of St. Johannes when his name was mentioned. The publicity that centered about the girl resulted from the very exotic phenomena of marks of biting upon her arms, etc. She became the subject of intensive observation and experimentation by many well-known scientists and numerous phenomena were observed under strict control.

Case after case followed and it is obviously impossible to list even a fraction of the known examples. Without doubt, for every instance that reaches the notice of the investigator, there are ten that are never heard of. For example, during the early part of 1964, I received word of a definitely genuine poltergeist case, but due to religious scruples, and the like, it proved impossible to gain an entrée and study the phenomena.

Father Thurston relates a particularly interesting case that occurred in India, March 3 to 19, 1920, which was very well attested and received considerable attention in the Hindu press. Fires were started and an apparition was seen which answered a question, saying, "Why, Father." An extreme aversion was shown for the many religious articles and symbols used in a desperate effort to rid the home of the unwanted, infesting force. Threatening messages were also discovered on the wall.

The extremely well-known rock-throwing case that became a sensation at the town of Chico, California, in the year 1922 has become the subject of many articles in books, and beyond mentioning that the aerial bombardment generally centered on two adjoining warehouses, little else need be said. A strange additional feature of this case is that in 1878 a fall of small fish fell from a cloudless sky on Chico, and in 1885, a large object, several tons in weight, fell near the town. To further complicate the case, strange noises, or explosions were reported in the sky over Oroville, a town near Chico.

To choose more or less at random, the *Los Angeles Herald*, July 12, 1939, described a ghostly intruder that threw little images, nails, tacks, pieces of tiles, and other objects in a small print shop owned by Mr. and Mrs. Harry Park in Los Angeles.

A report was included in the *Waterbury Republican* describing an attack of falling stones upon a building at Bethlehem, Conn., 1953, and stating that the rock bombardment had lasted for about two years.

Quite a stir was made in Seaford, Long Island, in 1958, when an actually rather mild disturbance became the subject of enormous publicity and public attention. Various objects were said to have been hurled about and bottle caps were removed from bottles. Different authorities arrived at different answers regarding the authenticity of the case, primarily, I believe, because of the tendency of many researchers to refuse to accept the possibility that paranormal phenomena can exist.

Reviewing the history of the outbreak and the evidence presented, and in particular the observations of Detective Joseph Tozzi who witnessed a sugar bowl in the last part of its flight, there seems little doubt that genuine phenomena did occur. The house, incidentally, was blessed by a priest in an effort to quell the activities of the poltergeist, but to no avail.

It does seem a little ridiculous that the controversy still continues regarding the reality of such paranormal phenomena at this late date when the vast amount of evidence is considered, and the excellent observations made by major scientists of great repute are examined. For example, as is common knowledge, Sir William Barrett, F. R. S., while investigating a case in Ireland, heard paranormal knockings, and witnessed a pebble fall apparently from the ceiling within a room.

In Turin, Italy, Prof. Cesare Lombroso personally saw bottles break in a poltergeist-infested cellar with no one but himself present. Other phenomena were also reported.

These names are but two of many and will serve as examples of the witnesses that can be brought forward to verify the reality of the poltergeist.

Some Interesting Modern Cases

In Georgetown, British Guiana, during the month of March and the early part of April, 1960, a mysterious series of fires plagued a family, according to the *Los Angeles Times*. These events were obviously centered about a fifteen year old boy. Prayers had been offered, and, as usual, the phenomena still continued.

A rather odd example of paranormal rappings took place in October, 1962, in Nashville, Tennessee, which consisted entirely of knockings and rappings.

In 1960, I personally investigated a remarkable stone-throwing case in Lynwood, California, and another even more remarkable example in 1962-1963 in Big Bear City, also in California.

It is clearly impossible to give a really comprehensive account of the vast number of cases that have taken place over the years, as we have remarked, much less keep up with the new examples that continually occur. As a result, I have very briefly touched on the history of the poltergeist, and attempted only to give a sufficient number of better known cases of the past and of recent times. Though many excellent cases have, of necessity, been omitted, still the list does give a general picture of the varied and truly exotic phenomena that has been encountered with the poltergeist.

CHAPTER HIGHLIGHTS

The poltergeist is as old as history. Cases were recorded in Ancient Egypt, Greece and Rome. Famed disturbances were noted during the Middle Ages, the Rennaissance, etc., and are equally active today. Hauntings followed the colonists to the New World and current cases are being investigated now in the interests of science.

chapter 3

Mysterious Rock-Falls Caused by Poltergeists

Stone Throwing Is Typical

One of the commonest effects to be found with the poltergeist is the mysterious stone-throwings and falls that have been reported for hundreds of years. These peculiar and unexplained happenings share with paranormal rappings and knockings the honor of being perhaps the most readily found manifestation with our ghostly visitant.

Excellent Evidence Plentiful

The evidence is so very plentiful and of such excellent quality that it seems near-ridiculous that this phenomenon remains in dispute and is generally ignored by the scientific world. There is little doubt that the near-fanatical dislike for the field as a whole stems from the completely mechanistic philosophy that came into full flower in the late 1800's. It still holds sway today, though disguised by verbal acrobatics. Although the very rigid push-pull determinism of the past has evolved into the more sophisticated, fluid theories of the present, the utter materialism of the Victorians continues to hold the field. Paranormal phenomena is not yet a polite subject for the orthodox, scientific parlor. As a result, the poltergeist remains outside the field of "official" science, and will remain so for a number of years, I fear. I say that the poltergeist does exist: Sir William Barrett wrote, *Stones are frequently thrown, but no one is hurt; I myself have seen a large pebble drop apparently from space in a room where the only culprit could have been myself, and certainly I did not throw it.*

I have personally observed more than three cases involving poltergeist, or haunting effects, and have investigated others on the spot where the evidence was conclusive for paranormal falls of stones and other manifestations. As a result, my viewpoint is influenced completely by these experiences, and I see little reason to doubt other well-attested cases. The phenomena are simply too plentiful to dismiss, and the evidence is enormous in extent.

Frequently, stone throwings may be the only phenomenon present during a case, and may also be found with other types of effects. In many cases, stones have dropped into rooms in spite of the fact that solid ceilings should have intervened, and in other cases the falls of rocks occurred entirely outside of the afflicted houses. Still other examples have been reported as happening in fields and open ground.

Stone-throwings and stone-falls can really be separated into two categories. One type is strictly of paranormal origin easily attributed to the poltergeist, and the other is the product of a natural, though at present, unknown process. For the purpose of illustration, a number of cases will be described; some of an earlier vintage, and some quite recent.

One of the earlies examples on record occurred in 1170 A.D. when the hermitage of St. Godric was said to have been the subject of a bombardment by stones and other objects.

Centuries later, the *London Daily Mail,* reported on May 6, 1910, that from 10 o'clock until noon, May 4, rocks shot up from the ground and loud detonations

43

were heard. The paper remarked that it was thought that a volcanic crater was in the process of formation, but volcanoes are not known in Spain where the event took place.

San Diego, California Stoning

A rock-throwing was reported by the *San Diego Union and Evening Tribune* in the Sept. 10, 1962 issue, which described the mysterious pelting with no apparent knowledge of the poltergeist concept. The word "poltergeist" does not appear in the article, nor does any suggestion of paranormal action find print.

As reported, rocks and an occasional clod of dirt had been striking the home of Mr. and Mrs. K. S., and the barrage had started one day during the last week of August, and was intermittent in nature. For four days, between the hours of 10 A.M. to 3 P.M., and from 7:30 P.M. until 10 P.M. the rock-throwing had been active.

Mrs. S., who was struck with rocks on the back and shoulder while hanging out clothes, said her seventeen-month old baby, her son's friend, and a friend of hers, had been hit. The blows were painful, but not serious.

A crank telephone call was received, an incident not surprising, informing the family that if the children were given away the people of outer space would cease their unwelcome attentions. Apparently the crews of "flying-saucers" are dependent upon a stone-age technology.

The article continued telling that the police had "gone underground" in their efforts to catch the culprit "who may be using a large slingshot in a tree" to fire stones the size of walnuts and pieces of dirt at the S. home.

A photograph was included which pictured a boy 15,

pointing out to his five-year-old brother a hole in a play helmet. Judging from the photograph, the helmet seems to have been made of plastic, in which case the rock that made the hole must have possessed considerable velocity.

There were several children involved, providing a splendid choice for an inadvertant poltergeist-medium. It also was very apparent that the poltergeist was given to physical violence, at least to the degree that several people were painfully struck, including the baby. Again, it becomes noticeable that the poltergeist is not a harmless and humorous prankster, but a potentially malignant power.

Disturbance in Pennsylvania

In May, 1963, *The Philadelphia Inquirer* included articles telling of a typical rock-throwing case that occurred in Pennsylvania, disturbing the home of Mr. J. S. According to the *Inquirer*, the police had made extensive investigations of the case and were unable to solve it.

I received a letter from Mr. S. in which he stated,

. . . I could add that it lasted for about six weeks, off and on. It wasn't until one of the policemen was almost hit while investigating that the papers gave it notice. After the first write-up, just a few rocks fell that day. Less the following day. After the fourth consecutive day that the article appeared in the papers, the stones stopped falling, and we haven't had any since. We never found out who did it and how it was done.

Revealingly, no mention was made whatsoever regarding the possibility of a paranormal force at work in the articles that I obtained, and, in fact, an editorial was written referring the outbreak to the activities of juveniles, and the ever-present "ballistic device."

Mysterious Slingshots and Catapults

One of the most remarkable things about the entire subject of falling rocks is a phenomenon which can be termed—The Great Slingshot, or Catapult Mystery. These ubiquitous devices have a very long and respectable history. In spite of the information that has become quite plentiful, explaining and describing poltergeist phenomena, slingshots and catapults are regularly and predictably trotted out to explain a good percentage of the new cases that are constantly occurring. A very interesting history could be written describing the appearance of these never-discovered gadgets. To my immediate knowledge, a slingshot, or catapult, has never been found in all the great number of rock-throwing cases that have been reported. No doubt, these devices are rarer than the poltergeist itself.

The *Waterbury Republican* described a case that pelted buildings at Bethlehem, Connecticut, in 1953. The newspaper told how stones dropped upon the house of Mr. M. H. for about two years. The phenomena were intermittent and not constant. At first, Mr. H. suspected that children were tossing rocks from a hill nearby, but upon investigation was unable to find a suspect. Local police were called in, but were completely baffled. One significant observation was made by a constable who commented on the abnormally slow fall of the flying rocks. Though the constable was unaware of the significance of his observation, a common and typical effect of such cases is that the various missiles that are so thrown frequently fly through the air with a velocity much less than would normally be expected.

An example of an earlier period was given in the *Rand Daily Mail*, May, 1922, which told of a fall of stones that lasted for several months in South Africa. According to the newspaper report, a Mr. Neaves, living near Roodeport, had his house pelted by showers of rocks, and finally went to the police for aid. They investigated the case thoroughly and found nothing amiss. They did notice, however, that the rocks fell vertically, which made fraud difficult. Completely baffled, the police finally announced that a culprit had been found and that he had confessed that he had thrown the stones while concealed in a nearby outhouse. Previously, the outhouses had been searched and it seems rather obvious that the "exposure" was arranged for police "convenience."

A fall of stones described in the *London Times*, Jan. 13, 1843, provides us with a very typical case, but also gives us an added phenomenon of a most strange nature. Two small girls saw rocks falling about them, and reported that they fell very slowly. The abnormally slow fall is a well-known effect of the poltergeist, and we will meet it again in the Big Bear City outbreak. There was, however, another fantastic effect—an upward pull, or current, which seemed to draw the children into it. This peculiar manifestation was also found in another poltergeist case.

Oddities With Thrown Objects

Numerous examples exist where stones have fallen, or have been thrown, inside of houses, and closed rooms. Stones have been thrown with uncanny and unerring accuracy through a hole in a window, and stones both hot and cold have fallen or "floated" down. These last two attributes are again nearly traditional effects found in "classic" poltergeist cases.

Telekinetic sights of objects have frequently betrayed the same strange, slow motion. In fact, it has been observed that objects engaged in these reported aerial acrobatics have given all indications of having been picked up, carried about, and at times, hurled by invisible hands. Instead of suggested unseen forces, such as "magnetic fields," and other vague and unsatisfactory theoretical explanations, it has been remarked that perhaps the poltergeist-force created hands to hold, carry and throw objects about. This theory does possess certain advantages, for it is indeed difficult to see how a "force" can manage the complicated motions that have occurred. It seems difficult to imagine a "force" picking something up to carry it about, or at times throwing an object with marvelous aim. Of course, to some, one formidable objection to this thought is the temptation to carry it to its logical conclusion and theorize the existence of a spirit conducting such activities. However repugnant the theory may be, or however attractive it may be, nevertheless, such attributes have nothing whatsoever to do with the truth or falsity of the theory.

A Stone-Throwing in New Zealand

A splendid example of the stone-throwing poltergeist was the subject of numerous articles in several New Zealand publications. The case occurred at a guest house in Wellington in March, 1963.

The unearthly bombardment began at 9:30 P.M. when a penny smashed a window in the lodge. Immediately other pennies, and then rocks began to smash windows and crash against the building. A party of lodgers who had just returned from coffee and were chatting on the veranda when the missiles flew dangerously close, took cover in the kitchen at the rear of the house. The police arrived upon the strange scene and so began a very extensive investigation of the rockfall which lasted for several days.

Mrs. A. kindly replied to a letter of interrogation and I include an excerpt from this letter.

. . . My husband and self are at a loss as to know why people . . . have blamed the trees which we think are about 100 years old. We have had all sorts of suggestions, but after the trees were cut right down, no more stone-throwing. It certainly gives us food for thought. . . .

You can see the size of the stones in the pictures, some of which were ordinary rocks such as on our foot-paths, and some had a lot of concrete on them.

The police said they had warned someone who was doing it for fun, but I don't believe that. We had radar set-up, search lights, everything to help, but, alas, the stones continued to arrive with terrific force . . .

Several large trees played a strange part in the disturbance. After the rock-throwing had begun a Samoan insisted on speaking to Mr. A. alone and told him that when the trees, which had previously been cut down, were cut the trunks had been left too high and represented something evil. The visitor implored Mr. A. to have the tree trunks cut down to ground level.

Later, an elderly Maori woman visited the afflicted house and also remarked that the manner in which the trees had been cut down was responsible for the disturbance. She then proceeded to perform a form of exorcism both inside and outside the house, and when finished announced that "there would be no trouble from evil spirits, and there would be no more stone-throwing."

Again, we have an example of the curious and often noticed connection between the phenomena found with the poltergeist, and witchcraft. Evil spirits and exorcism still play their ancient roles in the drama of the poltergeist.

Two Remarkable California Rock-Throwings

Two remarkable rock-throwing cases, both of which I personally investigated, took place in California. One, the Lynwood Poltergeist, occurred on September 9th and 10th, 1960, and the other, the Big Bear City Rock-Throwing Case, was first reported to the police, July 19, 1962, and lasted until November 16 of the same year. Both cases were "explained" by the catapult and slingshot theory, as can be imagined, and the following chapters will give a somewhat detailed history of these truly classic examples.

Strange Similarities of Stone-Throwings

As an end to this chapter devoted to the peculiar phenomena of stone-throwings, it might be well to mention that there are a number of odd practices found throughout the world which very possibly have a connection with our mysterious rocks.

One of the strange practices is the pelting of graves of persons of evil life—those accused of black magic, bandits, murderers, and the like—with the intention of frustrating the malignant ghosts haunting the tainted sites. The missiles used are stones, clods, or sticks, and these actions are found in various parts of Africa, Syria, Pomerania and West Prussia. The belief that a malignant spirit haunts the burial spot and the use of stones and other missiles are certainly reminiscent of the poltergeist, and may actually have come about as the result of contact with poltergeist phenomena by ancient primitives.

CHAPTER HIGHLIGHTS

Stone-throwings are a very typical poltergeist effect. Evidence for paranormal bombardments is plentiful and of excellent quality—a rock-throwing in San Diego, California; a stoning in Pennsylvania. Slingshots and catapults are repeatedly invoked as natural explanations, but are never found. Abnormal "floating" motions and actions of thrown objects are typical of poltergeist action.

chapter 4

Pseudo-Stone Throwings

False Rock-Throwings Occur

Interestingly, there exists a type of stone-fall, and in fact, falls of all types of objects, that to some extent parallel the stone-throwings of poltergeist origin. Many such examples are given in the works of Charles Fort, and he suggested that perhaps such oddities are due to a kind of "cosmic poltergeist."

Practically everything imaginable has at one time or another fallen from the skies, and many such incidents have been ably reported, and have had numerous witnesses. As is well-known, fish have fallen, as have pieces

of coal, various types of organic material, lumps of iron
—not meteoric in nature—ice, vast amount of leaves, and
the like.

A Mysterious Rock-Fall in Iowa

A case quite typical occurred in Iowa, and as it presents a perfect example of these strange rock-falls I will
give it in some detail. This case came to my attention
by way of an article in the *Cedar Rapids Gazette*,
August 16, 1962, which very briefly told of curious com-
plications which plagued a fishing trip of a Mr. Hasenbank. While fishing, he first encountered a mysterious
rain of pebbles which fell into the water. He immediately thought that some boys might have been throwing
them as a prank, but after looking around found no one
nearby.

He changed his fishing ground to another spot and
while there rocks pelted the car in which he was sitting.
Upon returning home he told his wife and daughter
about the strange events, and they told him that they
had heard hail, or what they thought was hail, hitting
the windows of their home. They went outside and
again the pebbles began to fall from a clear sky. The
stones fell "like hail."

Mrs. Russell Lovell collected a number of the pebbles
and showed them to a neighbor who was interested in
geology. He checked them with a Geiger counter for
possible radiation but none was found.

The stones were finally sent to the State University
of Iowa for study which pronounced them to be simply
pebbles of limestone, quartz and igneous rock, slightly
water-worn, and used for road gravel.

I found this short article quite interesting and wrote
to Mr. Hasenbank requesting further information, and
he, in turn, gave my letter to Mr. Russell Lovell who

replied. Mr. Lovell's letter was very informative and furnished considerable insight into the reluctance of many to make such events known publicly. He gave such an excellent account of the fall that I believe it should be set out here with the exception of minor deletions as follows:

Dear Sir:

I am writing in regard to the rocks that fell from the sky last fall. I live next door to Henry Hasenbank and as they did not want to write, they let me read your letter and asked me to write . . . I am the person that started all the publicity. The day the rocks fell they (Mr. and Mrs. Hasenbank) didn't want to tell anyone about it because they were afraid people would make fun of them.

My wife and I and a neighbor . . . saw these rocks. I told Mr. Hasenbank they should send the rocks to the laboratory at Iowa City, Iowa, but they didn't want to, so I sent a few of them to the lab. The answer I got back was: "They are simply pebbles of limestone, quartz and igneous rock, slightly water-worn, and probably used for road gravel."

We had a freak storm the night before and I thought the rocks might be from that, but these rocks were not seen until the afternoon of August 16, 1962. There were no clouds in the sky nor any wind. Mr. Hasenbank first noticed the rocks about 3 P.M. at Oxford Junction while fishing. He said that he saw them hitting the water and for a time thought some boys might be throwing them. After looking around, however, he found no one else in the area. He said he didn't pay much attention, however, and as the fish weren't biting, he went on to Massilon, Iowa, to fish.

There the rocks fell on his car while he was sitting in it. There was another witness from there who saw the rocks fall from the sky. Mr. Hasenbank decided to go home, bewildered about this, and told his wife and daughter about the rocks. Thinking they would say he imagined it, (by the way, Mr. Hasenbank had his ten-year-old grandson with him that afternoon) he was surprised when his wife said that she had heard something like hail hitting the windows of their house.

The Hasenbanks told my wife about the rocks falling from the sky and she thought that they had lost their minds until, while they were there telling her, she saw the rocks fall too. She picked up a rock and brought it home to show me.

It was about 5:30 P.M. by then, so I had a big laugh, too, but after suppper I went over to Hasenbanks to find out about this and when I was almost up to Mr. Hasenbank one fell in a pan that he had with him. I told him to give me the rock. While we were talking his daughter and grandson joined us and every few minutes the rocks would fall. Some would hit us on the shoulder and arms. They did not come straight down, but at an angle of 45°, like snowflakes. It seemed they were in a path about 50 feet wide, but how long I do not know. This kept up until about dark. On the same day some people reported that rocks had fallen where they were having a Ladies' Aid about twenty miles away, straight southwest.

The next night, two blocks west of Hasenbanks, on the same side of the street, a lady told us rocks had fallen on her house, but she said before it happened there seemed like an explosion. She has the rocks to prove it, too. They were in her eaves' spouts. She didn't want to tell anyone about it because she was afraid people would not believe her. One of her neighbors told me about this, so I went over and talked to her about the rocks.

After I sent the rocks to Iowa Geological Survey at Iowa City, they called up the Cedar Rapids Gazette to *find out if anybody at Clarence had reported it. The WMT-TV at Cedar Rapids . . . came down. The TV man took some rocks with him to be analyzed, and that night on TV, they showed pictures of us, but all they said was that some kids were shooting the rocks in slingshots . . . The next morning I was ashamed to go downtown to get my mail because I was afraid the people would make fun of me, but to my surprise the people were mad too . . . There was a nice article about the rocks in the Cedar Rapids Gazette in August, 1962.*

This is all I can tell you about the rocks. I am sending you a few along with this letter . . . If there are any more questions, I will be glad to help you.

I wrote in answer to Mr. Lovell's very descriptive letter asking if it might be possible to obtain corroborating statements from other witnesses. Mrs. Lovell kindly replied, telling me of her experiences with the stone-fall. She also sent the signatures of Mr. and Mrs. Henry Hasenbank and their daughter, Velma, signifying that they had witnessed the rockshowers.

Certainly a remarkable feature of this happening was the great number of pebbles that fell. Judging from Mr. Lovell's letter, the number must have been enormous.

Another remarkable characteristic was the large area affected. It is possible that the rocks may have dropped into a comparatively small area at any given time, but still the zone involved was at least twenty miles in length.

One oddity, however, was the reported explosive sound that was said to have happened before a fall. Here, we do have a rather suspicious phenomenon reminiscent of the explosions so often heard in true poltergeist cases. For the moment we will ignore this interesting parallel and present the case as a splendid example of the mysterious sky-falls that have so often been observed and reported.

Charles Fort, of course, included great numbers of

such happenings in his works, and such effects have received the fitting title—*Fortean Phenomena*.

In spite of the mystery that largely surrounds these strange falls of objects, I am convinced that they are of "natural" origin, and are completely free of paranormal effects. Rev. Guy J. Cyr, S.M. of the Sacred Heart Rectory in Lawrence, Mass., has written a very interesting paper in which he advances a theory outlining a physical mechanism for such phenomena, and it is well worth consideration and study. There is much about such sky-falls that is certainly not explained, and there are falls that seem to border on the paranormal, but in general this phenomena can be considered to be of normal, if mysterious, origin, even though it does at times appear similar to stone-falls, and stone-throwings of paranormal origin.

CHAPTER HIGHLIGHTS

Pseudo or non-paranormal rock-falls occur. A typical and recent example was in Iowa where large numbers of pebbles fell over a great area with no explanation of the phenomena. A famous researcher, Charles Fort has listed many mysterious falls of varied materials other than rocks which are also unexplainable.

chapter 5

The Big Bear City Poltergeist

A Personal Investigation

My attention was drawn to this remarkable rock-fall case in quite a domestic manner, certainly free from romance and Gothic atmosphere. On the morning of November 10, 1962, while reading the *Los Angeles Times*, my wife noticed an article describing an apparent poltergeist case which was in progress and remarked, "You wanted poltergeist phenomena, well, here it is." With these words she handed me the newspaper and I immediately plunged into the story of an amazing rock-fall that was presumably still continuing.

The article began with the promising title, *"Pelted Day and Night,* followed by the tantalizing sub-title, *Mysteriously Floating Stones Bombard House, Rout Residents.* According to the writer, stones had been "floating" down from the sky for four months, and had been bombarding a mountain home in Big Bear City, California. San Bernardino Sheriffs had investigated the mystery for most of that time and were still thoroughly baffled.

A Deputy Sheriff said, *None of our officers have ever seen the stones fall from the sky. Until we do, we'll have to assume some human agency is involved.* He further remarked that the police had conducted thorough and extensive searches in the area surrounding the disturbed home immediately after it had been pelted by the mysterious rocks. They were never able to discover a suspect. *Reliable witnesses in the neighborhood have told us they have seen the stones as they floated down from the sky.*

The article went on to say that a one-story house became the focal point for a mysterious fall, or throwing, of stones after the occupant and his family moved in on June 15th. Soon after, the occupant notified the officers at the Big Bear Substation that rocks were pelting his home.

Stones were found by deputy sheriffs, some four inches in length, weighing from one to four ounces. Some of the windows in the afflicted house were smashed by stones, and the deputies were told that one of the Lowe children had been struck by a falling rock.

On October 13 a rock hit the hood of the Sheriff's patrol car while deputies were at the house investigating the mystery. On Halloween night, a stone passed near a deputy sheriff and struck the house. The occupants moved to another house that night.

The stones struck the house about four times a day at unpredictable intervals, and sometimes, the occupants said, they fell from a bright blue sky.

Trying to find a "natural" answer for the strange fall of rocks, the occupant theorized that a strong wind blowing across a height called Rebel Ridge (a ski area about one-tenth of a mile away) picked up the stones and dropped them on his house. A deputy sheriff in turn stated, *I don't think that's the answer; we haven't had that much wind.*

The house that the occupants left gained three new tenants who were employed at a ski area nearby. Near the end of the news article comparison was made with the famous rock-fall that occurred in Chico, California.

The next day, November 11, the *Los Angeles Times* included another article again describing the disturbance at Big Bear City, which, more or less, was devoted to an interview with the present occupant.

He told how he and another person had dinner with the former occupant in the cabin before they moved and were jokingly informed that the house was haunted.

Soon after, the new occupant experienced the fall of stones and remarked, *One time my car was hit while I was standing right beside it. I had the sun-roof open and I heard a "plunk." I found the rock on the seat.*

He also observed that some of the stones were warm to the touch, and others were cold. He said that the stones were smooth, but not unlike other stones in the vicinity, and some weighed as much as nine ounces.

The San Bernardino County Sheriffs, who had been conducting an investigation for about three months, insisted that a human element was involved, but, *if a human force is moving the stones, officers haven't been able to track it down.*

The article further told how various officers had been in the cabin when rocks fell, and that two of their patrol cars had been slightly damaged by the strange missiles. The article concluded with the statement that stones had fallen both day and night and fell about every four days.

Naturally, being extremely interested, I immediately drove to the site. Big Bear City proved to be about 130 miles from my home in Los Angeles, and during the drive I wondered if this story would prove to be merely the result of misguided publicity, or simply mal-observation, as so many presumed psychical, or paranormal events turn out to be. I finally arrived at my destination in the afternoon. Big Bear City is a mountain resort community at an altitude of 7,500 feet and borders on a large lake. The entire area is forested with pine trees and was a very pleasant change from the city.

Interview With a Police Witness

I first called at the Big Bear Sheriff's Substation, and there met with a deputy sheriff who was extremely helpful, and as time went by, proved to be a very able investigator as well as a great aid to my studies. He related his experiences with the falling rock mystery, and mentioned that he had seen over twenty rocks actually strike, and had witnessed one window struck and shattered.

He described the searches in which he had participated, looking for possible suspects, and stated that none had ever been found. At the end of our discussion he said, *I don't think anything human is causing it.* And I must admit that neither do I.

After my interview with the deputy sheriff, I drove on to the cabin which is near the highway. The cabin is a typical resort home, situated in a large cleared area and the nearest house is several hundred feet away. There are other scattered homes and cabins nearby overshadowed by a few pine trees. The area is in turn surrounded by a pine forest. A hill named Rebel Ridge, which is used for a ski area, is about one-tenth of a mile from the cabin, and artificial snow is manufactured on the slope for the ski-run.

Two Witnesses Interviewed

I knocked at the door and met the occupants who were having dinner. They invited me to come in after I had stated my mission—the investigation of the rockfall. During our conversation I was told that they had moved into the cabin Halloween night and while helping the former occupants move out, stones began to fall.

During the course of the fall two windows were broken and the car window was shattered. A search was made by the police and neighbors, but the mystery persisted.

They remarked that during their occupancy of the disturbed cabin, many falls had taken place, and both had felt a number of the stones and discovered to their astonishment, that some were warm and others cold.

It appeared that during one bombardment a man was struck on the arm, but was not injured, and immediately afterward a "plunk" was heard and a stone fell through the open sun-roof of his car and came to rest on the seat.

Both men interviewed said the rocks that had been seen striking, or rocks that were known to have just struck, dropped in an abnormally slow fall, and hit with much less force than expected.

I was also told that the rock-falls were intermittent and none had fallen for the last four days.

Police Testimony

Both men went on to work and I remained at the cabin. While there, two Deputy Sheriffs arrived in a patrol car and we discussed the case at length. They described the rock-falls and the general history of the incident and furnished me with much valuable information.

A Sheriff's remarks provided an observation of considerable interest. He said that when at the cabin in answer to a call from the previous tenants, he had seen two rocks strike and bounce on the roof. The odd thing he noticed was that these stones made much less sound when they struck than normally expected. As he stated, *They didn't make enough noise.*

He then went inside the cabin and three or four stones fell in front of the building. The patrol car was also struck by a rock which hit hard enough to cause sparks to fly. He remarked that the injury to the car was much less than it should have been, considering the size of the rock and its fall.

On one occasion, five officers were standing near the front porch of the cabin, when a stone again hit the patrol car, and then other rocks fell, and it was the opinion of the two officers that some must have flown in at an angle.

Both officers admitted that no suspects had been found out and they were very baffled by the entire affair. I mentioned that I had investigated a very similar case, and referred to other cases of various types. I particularly noted that the officers were quite unfamiliar with the concept of poltergeist phenomena, and, in fact, the very word, "poltergeist."

The two sheriffs returned to their station and I drove back into the village for dinner. I returned in the early evening and stayed at the cabin until 8:00 P.M. While there several people arrived, quite a few of whom had witnessed previous falls.

A Slow-Falling Stone

Among the several onlookers with whom I discussed the case was one who had been present when rocks fell. He described one incident when a stone fell at about 6:30 P.M. and was seen in the beams of the porch and house lights. He stated that the rock had fallen at an angle, and, *it coasted down slow.* I questioned him very sharply regarding this point and he insisted that the rock's motion had been much too slow to have been normal. He first saw the rock when it was about ten or twelve feet from the ground, and it struck about the same distance from him. He also told me that he had previously picked up two stones during a fall and found that they were warm to the touch!

A short time later, the fourteen-year-old daughter of the previous occupant came to the cabin, having heard that I was there to study the rock-fall and its history. She related the various incidents that have been described and remarked that she had handled about fifteen of the stones and had found some hot, and others cold.

Another interesting observation of hers was she thought that perhaps some rocks had fallen prior to her family's occupancy of the cabin, June 15, 1962. The reason she suspected this was that she had seen a large number of stones about the yard appearing much the same as they did after a fall. At any rate, the possibility that rocks had previously fallen does exist, though perhaps it is a bit remote.

My Personal Experience at Big Bear

I patrolled the cabin and immediate grounds, steadily watching for any suspicious actions on the part of the few onlookers that came and went, but saw nothing whatsoever that suggested possible fraud. The night was truly beautiful, and a large, frosty moon shone above the trees. However, the night was also bitterly cold, and my watch became more and more uncomfortable until at last it turned into a true ordeal. Poltergeist hunting is fascinating, surprising and occasionally rewarding, but it also can have drawbacks, and the cold of the night certainly fell into that category.

At 7:10 P.M. I was startled to hear an object strike the ground about fifteen feet from me. The impact was unmistakable. Unfortunately, in spite of the full, brilliant moon, I simply could not find the missile as it had fallen into a dense clump of weeds that happened to have been in a deep shadow. As a consequence, I cannot actually say that I saw a rock fall, or strike, but taking everything into consideration, the possibility for the unseen object to have been a falling stone is certainly strong. I saw nothing in the least of a suspicious nature during my patrol and no trees were close enough to have dropped a pine cone or a branch.

A reporter admitted that he had also experienced a similar incident on the grounds surrounding the cabin. He heard rocks fall on the roof of a shed about one hundred feet from the cabin, but did not actually see them hit.

At 8:00 o'clock it became so cold that I decided that inasmuch as nothing else had happened, and it seemed that I could do little more to further my investigation, I should return home. I must admit the return drive in a warm, heated car was most welcome.

In an effort to gain further evidence, I wrote to various people who had been involved in the rock case, and in particular, began corresponding with Deputy Sheriff Jack H. Cox of the Big Bear Substation. Sheriff Cox proved to be an excellent investigator and furnished me with much valuable information. He sent me a history of the police investigation of the case which proved to be of extreme value. Inasmuch as this history does give such a very clear picture of the entire case I will briefly summarize the account below.

Official Case History

The official history of the rock-fall began with a call from the occupants of the cabin on July 19, 1962, at 9:04 P.M., and the Sheriff went to the cabin. When he arrived he was told by the occupants that rocks had been thrown at their home and their children, and stones had been falling for the past two weeks. She also added the significant remark that footsteps had been heard on the roof after midnight, but no one had ever been found. These effects were the only other manifestations reported, and are, of course, very typical of the poltergeist. A little later, the same night, a private patrolman was asked to watch the cabin and surrounding area for any suspicious persons, and he in turn encountered the rocks as they fell upon the cabin again.

The Sheriff returned to the cabin August 10, and was informed that no rocks had fallen since the last incident, but a call was received by the Sheriff's station a short time later which told of further falls of stones. Two officers answered the call, and while at the cabin, two rocks hit the building. A search was again made but nothing suspicious was found.

When answering a call on October 13, Sheriff Cox and two other officers were informed that one of the occupant's children had made the call from a neighbor's house and that rocks had bombarded this structure. The officer's patrol car was struck by a stone and a search was made with the usual negative results. Sheriff Cox was told that actually many rock falls had occurred both night and day, and that the rocks at times felt both hot and cold.

Halloween night, October 31, furnished a very lively evening, for Sheriff Cox saw about twenty rocks fall, some straight down and others at an angle, and noticed that they came from all directions. He noticed that the *rocks seemed to follow the beams of the flashlights that were in the area.* He also noted that the rocks seemed to follow the occupant's children wherever they went.

Sheriff Cox made another call at the cabin November 16, and was told by the tenants that stones had fallen but were diminishing in number.

The *Big Bear Lake News-Pictorial,* November 21, printed an article describing later developments of the rock case, and included a report from a local citizen who said that a rock hit the top of her car in the Rebel Ridge area last Friday night around 9 P.M. Riding with her daughter and two friends, she said that the rock hit the top of the car hard and loud enough so that she suspected there would be a rather large dent in the car's body. Examination the following day disclosed no such dent.

Many Theories Offered as Explanation

As always happens in such cases, many theories are offered attempting to explain away the mystery of the phenomena. In this case the inevitable catapult and slingshot were brought to the fore, and so were powerful winds picking up rocks from the nearby Rebel Ridge ski-slope. The machines used for making artificial snow came in for their share, and so did a hypothetical newly-formed natural gas vent.

Both sensible and silly theories proved totally and completely inadequate, and the paranormal nature of the stonefall still remains the obvious and correct answer, both by the fact that the various investigations of the case were unable to discover fraud, or normal causes, and by comparison with other well-known examples of this type of phenomena.

The public investigation and general public observation took care of catapults and slingshots, and the powerful winds presumably capable of carrying rocks would have necessarily been of such tremendous velocity that no house would have remained standing in Big Bear City. We need not even mention the fact that for such a selective wind to deposit the rocks on such a comparatively small target would have been in the nature of a major miracle.

The hypothetical gas vent is, obviously, ridiculous. How such an amazing phenomenon could have escaped the notice of those living about the area is totally inconceivable, and, again, the incredible ability of the missile-firing gas vent to select a small target would have required another majestic miracle.

Actually, the only theory advanced that had any real thought behind it was the suggestion that the high pressure nozzles used to create the artificial snow might have been utilized to fire the stones. However, this suggestion was soon disposed of when I determined that the snow-machinery was only used during the day and had only been in operation since the latter part of October. The rocks, as we know, had fallen both night and day, and had fallen as early as July 19.

The nature of the falls, the peculiar behavior and slow velocity of the rocks, and the temperature oddities of the stones, etc, all are typical characteristics of poltergeist phenomena. In view of the evidence offered by the many witnesses—I have only listed a few—I can only conclude that paranormality has been well-established. The incident is, in my opinion, a near perfect example of typical rock-throwing phenomena, and is truly a classic one.

CHAPTER HIGHLIGHTS

A personal study of the stoning of a mountain home was made by the author. Newspaper articles described the case; a police investigator was interviewed. Two residents of the disturbed home were questioned. Two police investigators were interviewed. A witness mentioned seeing a "slow falling" stone and felt two abnormally warm rocks. Various "normal" theories were advanced, but all lacked plausible proof. Evidence for paranormal activity for rock-falls in Big Bear City is plentiful.

chapter 6

The Lynwood Poltergeist

A Used Car Lot Bombarded

I discovered this rock-throwing case at Lynwood, California, in much the same manner as the Big Bear City case. While reading the Saturday morning edition of a California paper September 10, 1960, I noticed an article with the intriguing heading, *Rocks Pelt Used Car Lot in Lynwood.* I immediately read on and discovered that according to the report a mysterious bombardment of a used car lot had occurred the previous day. Generally, the news account read as follows:

LYNWOOD, SEPTEMBER 9, 1960.

A modern-day David leveled his anger and his sling at a used car lot, hurling almost 200 egg-sized rocks at the business in a day-long attack that 18 policemen couldn't stop.

Was it a disgruntled car buyer?

"That's what we first thought," said a police sergeant. "But we asked the owner and he couldn't tell us anyone that had been mad lately. Now, we don't know who, why, or how."

All available officers were dispatched to the scene of

the rock attack. Although they patrolled with binoculars and walkie-talkies, they didn't have any luck. They began a house-to-house search for the stone-thrower late today.

One employee of the auto lot was hit by one of the stones and at least two cars were damaged, police said. The barrage started at 9:30 A.M. and ended punctually at 4:30—just when the house-to-house hunt started.

"That man can sure shoot," said a policeman who spent almost all day trying to solve the mystery. "Those rocks are coming from at least a block away and they are all hitting within a radius of fifty feet."

Officers theorized the rock-bomber must be using a sling, a slingshot, or catapult of some sort. One policeman said he thought the rocks were coming from at least three blocks away.

The next day, a newspaper report included the following information:

SEPT. 11, 1960
Suspect held in Car-Lot Barrage.
The nuts, bolts, and egg-sized rocks that had been raining down on a Lynwood car lot since Friday stopped yesterday afternoon after the arrest of a suspect, police said.

Police booked the suspect . . . in Lynwood jail, on a charge of obstructing officers in the line of duty.

Officers who were staked out opposite the lot reported they saw the suspect emerge from the office carrying a rock, look around, then pound the side of the car with it. After that, he reported another rock had landed.

"We're still convinced that someone else was catapulting rocks into the lot," a police officer said yesterday.

"Some fell Friday and this morning that the suspect couldn't have been responsible for. He was standing next to officers when the rocks landed."

According to the owner of the lot, the rocks began falling at 9:30 A.M. Friday at three-minute intervals. After two hundred rocks had landed, nuts, bolts and other pieces of iron began winging in with a flat trajectory, like a baseball line drive.

Three employees, including the suspect claimed they had been hit. Ten cars were slightly damaged.

My Personal Investigation at Lynwood

Assuming that there was a good possibility that the rock-throwing had been of paranormal origin. I drove to Lynwood, a town on the fringe of Los Angeles. I arrived at the lot at 3:00 P.M. and met the manager of the lot, who said that he had been present during the stone shower. He described the fall of the rocks, and other objects, and the general history of the case in some detail.

I noticed ten missiles in a row on the lot office inner window ledge, eight of which were stones, and two a nut and a bolt. The largest rock was about the size of a hen's egg, and upon request, I was given two. There was nothing unusual about the rocks and the nut and bolt appeared normal.

I was shown about the car lot, including a wooden garage which was used as a shop, and was shown a wooden wall which had been hit upon the inside during the bombardment, leaving an indentation about one eighth of an inch deep. The depth of the indentation and the relative hardness of the wood indicated that the stone had struck with considerable speed.

After I had finished my inspection of the car lot, I drove to the Lynwood Police Station and met and questioned the officer in charge who had directed the investigation of the mysterious rock-throwing. He discussed the case in detail, telling how eighteen policemen had searched the surrounding neighborhood as well as the lot in an attempt to apprehend the hypothetical marksman using a hypothetical catapult. No such suspect, or device, was found.

He insisted that the suspect was definitely not responsible for the shower of rocks, and told me how at one time the suspect was under strict police surveillance when the rocks were actually falling. He also described how he had the suspect under observation with the aid of binoculars and was thereby able to see that rocks fell completely apart from any actions of the suspect.

It was stated that no evidence was forthcoming connecting the suspect to the rock-throwing other than one minor incident that he had observed while using the binoculars. He saw the suspect leave the lot office, pick up a rock and strike a car with it. Little importance was placed on this event inasmuch as the suspect had been proven innocent when other rocks had fallen. The only evidence found was strictly "circumstantial," which consisted of the fact that inasmuch as the suspect was known to have been innocent, therefore a confederate must have been in the neighborhood using a catapult. This belief rested upon the incontrovertible fact that rocks do not normally fly through the air unaided. I fear that the police official was quite unacquainted with poltergeist lore. He did admit, however, that it was impossible to uncover the hypothetical confederate.

I asked if the suspect had any previous police record,

and if any abnormal incidents connected with him had ever been reported. I was told that the suspect was completely free from any police record, and no previous unusual events had ever been noted.

I then asked if the case was considered "baffling," and he replied that he thought it was and it had definitely not been solved. He still believed that a confederate had been using a catapult, however, but had managed to evade the police search.

A police aide telephoned the suspect's mother two days later and questioned her at length about her son, and the rock case in general. Her English was quite limited and consequently the interrogation proved unproductive. She did, however, remark that her son was unmarried, but had worked on other car lots, and that nothing out of the ordinary had ever happened before. She said that her son's jobs had not paid very well, and that he resented washing cars, working so very hard, and receiving small wages. She was asked several times if any abnormal noises, motions of objects, etc., had ever been noticed at home, but she replied that such had not been the case. She also remarked that her son had admitted hitting the car with a stone, but that he had maintained his innocence regarding the other falling rocks.

Interview With The Lot Owner

I telephoned the owner of the used car lot and questioned him at length regarding the various details of the rock-throwing. He said the suspect had worked for him for two days before the stone-shower occurred. He then remarked about the "terrific speed" that the rocks had manifested a number of times, and was very obviously impressed by this feature. I questioned him as to possible temperature oddities of the stones, but he answered that during the excitement no one had noticed. He said that near the end of the incident other types of objects were thrown as well as rocks.

The owner told me in considerable detail how the suspect had been in the car lot office with him, under strict observation when rocks fell outside the office building, and also stated that the suspect had been under police surveillance many times when stones had fallen. In fact, he insisted that the suspect was absolutely not responsible for the stone-throwing in the main, and was very emphatic regarding that point.

The owner told me how the suspect had left the office, reached down to pick up a small stone, and had thrown it at a car. The police who had been watching him with glasses, swooped down and took him into custody. It was the owner's opinion that this action of the suspect was on the order of a child's desire to take part in the exciting proceedings, and repeated his belief that he was not responsible for the strange bombardment.

The suspect was given a trial by jury which took place in the Compton Municipal Court in California.

Court Trial and Testimony

Various witnesses gave their testimony including several police officers who had taken part in the investigation. One officer described how he had arrived at the lot on the morning of September 9 when several rocks struck the garage at the rear of the lot. Asked if he had been able to determine the rock's source, he admitted that during the two-day period of investigation, and with as many as thirty police officers in the field, it had proved impossible to locate the origin of the stone.

Another police officer testified that he had been stationed in a nearby church tower, equipped with field glasses and a walkie-talkie sender and receiver to further the investigation. He told the court that when a rock struck the car lot this information was immediately relayed to him and he then searched the surrounding area for any suspicious person, or action. None was found.

A police official reported how he had seen the suspect pick up a stone and strike a car with it, which of course provided the legal justification for arresting him. In spite of this apparently damaging observation the police official in answer to the Defender's question, *Did you see any rocks being thrown?*, admitted that he had not.

The Prosecutor's final argument, and his evident lack of a real charge, and lack of evidence, placed him in a position of considerable difficulty. He remarked . . . *rocks fell on a car lot. The defendant has not been charged with throwing rocks per se, but he has been charged with obstructing officers in doing their duty.* His last statement was that the suspect, having found reporters and photographers on the lot investigating the disturbance, then created a disturbance with the rocks for the purpose of gaining publicity and attention.

Suspect Not Guilty

The defending attorney carefully pointed out that the entire affair was unfounded on fact for conviction. He reviewed the fact that thirty policemen in all had been called to investigate the mysterious fall of stones and were unable to discover their source. The point was made that the suspect had made absolutely no attempt to resist arrest and had gone willingly with the officers. The remarks were finally made that, due to the inability of the police to have stopped the rock-throwing, the lack of any real charge, *and due to the strange nature of the case, there must have been a "supernatural cause, a cosmic disturbance,"* responsible. *The jury returned a verdict of "not guilty."*

There is no doubt in my mind that the rock-throwing was a typical example of poltergeist phenomena. The fact that the very thorough police investigation did not reveal a natural cause behind the phenomena, and the fact that the various witnesses agreed that the suspect was innocent of the mystery, confirms the poltergeist theory.

A Comparative Case

The slingshot and catapult theories, of course, were the natural result of inability to solve the case. There was, as we have seen, absolutely no evidence whatsoever for the existence of a slingshot, or catapult, and the exhaustive police search confirmed their non-existence. For the purpose of comparison I include a very similar case that was reported in the *London Times*, April 27, 1872.

From four o'clock, Thursday afternoon, until half-past eleven, Thursday night, the houses 65 and 58 Reverdy Road, Barmondsey, were assailed with stones and other missiles, coming from an unseen quarter. Two children were injured, every window broken, and several articles of furniture were destroyed. Although there was a strong body of policemen scattered in the neighborhood, they could not trace the direction from whence the stones were thrown.

I merely picked this case at near-random, for as we have found, literally hundreds of such examples over the years have been witnessed and reported. The present offers no less evidence for the existence of such phenomena than does the past, and it is my belief that the number of such incidents not only equal the past, but far outnumber it. The increase in population explains quite well the growing amount of poltergeist cases, I am convinced.

CHAPTER HIGHLIGHTS

Newspaper accounts described the stoning of a used car lot. I examined the site and questioned many witnesses. The police captain who directed the investigation was interviewed. A suspect's innocence was established in a court trial. Valuable testimony was heard during the court trial that appears to indicate these rocks were paranormal and duplicated many times in various parts of the world—mysterious—but still incapable of explanation by conventional standards.

chapter 7

Poltergeist Rappings

Poltergeist Rappings Traditional

One of the most common effects to be found with hauntings and poltergeists is the phenomena of rapping. It exists in all degrees of intensity and has been reported to range from the most powerful and thunderous blows to faint, tiny tickings and tappings. Raps have occurred singly in the form of isolated blows and have also been heard in an entire series of fast drummings. The actual variety of raps that have been encountered is amazingly large, and these strange sounds have been described as very expressive at times.

Rappings have been traditionally coincidental with certain events, and in particular, death. This tradition is quite true. At other times they have apparently lacked any intelligent pattern, or purpose, as far as could be discovered. Experimental seances, of course, have provided many varieties of raps including those which have answered questions and which gave all indications of intelligence and awareness.

A Rapping Poltergeist

A very typical example of this phenomenon was described in several articles printed in a Tennessee newspaper, the case having begun in October, 1962, in Nashville. One article reads:

NOISY GHOST KEEPS FAMILY FROM SLEEP

. . ."It started four weeks ago," said Mrs. X. "It was knocking at the front of the house, and I thought it was one of the kids. I went to answer the door, but no one was there. It continued until morning. The second night we got guns.

"My husband thought I was imagining things. He took off from work and stayed here one night; that's when he started believing me. He shot a hole through the floor where it was knocking, but the noise just moved to another, and warmer, part of the floor.

"But if it's human, it ought to be dead—we've killed it enough times."

Then to Mrs. X's door trooped gas service men, electricians and policemen, with a certain Sherlock Holmes aplomb. They searched the house from the basement to the attic, found no case for the knocking, and left quietly . . .

Another article provided a few more details.

The ghost—or whatever it is—appeared at the X's home . . . exactly a month ago, knocking on the front and back doors and the house. Every night, sometimes as early as 6 P.M. and as late as 5 A.M., the loud, insistent knocks can be heard. The knocking continues for hours at times.

The police came and looked around. They sat in the living room and listened to the knocking. One night, two policemen staked out the house but could not catch the ghost.

Another night, as the ghost tapped on a window pane, a member of the X family fired a shot through the window. Unshaken, the ghost moved down the wall and tapped again.

Mr. X searched the attic and under the floor. No ghost.

One night, more than twenty high school football players sat on the front porch. They could hear the ghost but couldn't catch him.

"The ghost doesn't really bother us," says Mrs. X. "But the noise is so loud that none of us can sleep. We're all about to go crazy.

"We've tried everything, but we can't chase whatever it is away. And we've never been able to see it."

In still another article it was mentioned that the family included two teenage children; an eleven year old girl, and a fourteen year old boy. With the presence of these children, all the requirements were met for the creation of a poltergeist-haunting. The case is doubly interesting in that no other phenomena were noticed, and the only effects that occurred were the rappings. I will admit that the case could have been a rather hectic one indeed for an investigator, for not only would he have had to locate and follow the rappings, but also would have had to evade stray bullets.

A Door Smashed Open

Many cases involving rappings are described in Professor Camille Flammarion's *Haunted Houses* and I include an example that offered a single paranormal blow of great force.

In a house where jewelry of great value was frequently kept, footsteps were heard. This caused alarm and various attempts were made to trap the mysterious visitor, but to no avail. Glasses of water were placed upon the stairs in strategic positions and threads were stretched across the steps at intervals. These traps were found untouched and still the ghostly footsteps were heard walking up and down the stairs.

One evening after the writer of the original account had gone to bed at about 10:30 P.M., a solid oak door, which was described as having been two inches thick and locked in a most secure fashion, was smashed open by a tremendous blow or force. The lock was found in "closed" position, as well as the bolt, but still the door had been forced open by the great blow.

The writer mentioned that the footsteps and the startling opening of the door were not marked by any coincidental happening and that anticipated misfortune did not occur.

A Personal Experience of Mine

Over the years I have encountered several remarkable cases which did present genuine paranormal phenomena, but of a purely spontaneous nature. One of these which I have the good fortune to have witnessed occurred July 23, 1944, in a home in California. The house, I might add, did have a reputation for being haunted. Contrary to tradition no tragic events had happened. It was comparatively new, and had been purchased soon after it had been built. The house, therefore, had had no previous occupants.

I was sitting with Mrs. Y. in the breakfast room having coffee at about 5:30 P.M. No one else was in the house at the time, when suddenly a terrific blow struck the side of the house. It was so violent that my first thought was that an automobile had gone out of control and crashed into the building.

Almost immediately afterward a sound was heard that normally would have been attributed to a human hand scraping across the wire window screen, yet the wire did not bend under the pressure that should have been present. I was sitting about one yard, or less from the window and was looking directly at the source of the sound, and, presumably, the invisible thing that was scraping the screen. There simply was nothing in sight that could have either caused the blow on the side of the house, or the strange noises on the screen. To further simplify the situation, it was quite light outside.

The following day I carefully examined the window and general area. It was impossible for anyone to have reached the window, due to the fact that there was a thorny hedge three feet wide and twelve feet high, directly under the window and along the entire side of the house. It was only possible to have reached the window if a ladder had been placed against the hedge. A long, risky reach to the window might be possible, but in view of the fact that I was looking directly at the window as the unseen object raked the screen, this remote possibility was completely demolished. It must be added that the use of a long pole was also impossible for the same reason. There was and is no doubt in my mind that the strange incident was of paranormal cause. I will add that I witnessed another remarkable ghostly effect in the same house, but it will be described later.

I will again give an example from my own experience which occurred when I was about twelve years of age. It may be considered that due to the years that have elapsed my memory of the occasion may be faulty, and at times I have expressed the same criticism, but nevertheless I can assure the reader that my memory of this event is still vivid in every detail in my mind today.

A "Rapping" Desk is Clearly Heard

I was staying at my grandmother's home at the time and was busy in an adjoining room to where my grandmother and a friend were sitting. It was during the evening and they were discussing my grandfather, who had been dead for many years, when suddenly from his desk sounded three loud, distinct raps. Needless to say, all conversation ceased, and the comment was made that the raps were a signal, so to speak, from my grandfather.

The following day I carefully examined the desk, which was built into the wall, and noticed that it was completely sealed up with a wooden backing. It was quite impossible for a mouse, even if addicted to producing pseudo-psychical phenomena, to have entered the desk. I remember very clearly wishing to discover if such was possible. I also tested the desk for creaks, etc., and satisfied myself that the raps could not have been made by normal means. Apparently, I was beginning my pursuits in psychical research at an early age.

Raps that have portended misfortune, and in particular, death, are traditional, and can be said to be part of a universal folklore. Raps that have also warned of death occurring, or just past, are equally renowned. In such phenomena we have not only popular belief, but actual fact, and a great number of valuable examples exist furnishing just such effects. Many cases listing this type of phenomena also include other typical poltergeist happenings. It perhaps should be added that Prof. Flammarion, for example, considered that at times a spiritist element entered into these incidents.

Raps Heard at Death

Flammarion has listed numerous accounts of such rappings which were related to deaths in his various books, and a typical example was described by Mademoiselle Gabrielle Renaudot who was a member of the Astronomical Society of France and a well-known contributor to several scientific publications.

In 1906 a young woman died of tuberculosis. Her husband and a friend were present at her death and heard three loud blows upon the door of the room in which they were. The husband asked who had knocked and went to the door to open it. Receiving no answer, he returned to his dead wife's bed and once again heard three more violent knocks upon the door, and again went to the door and opened it. No one, of course, was there.

CHAPTER HIGHLIGHTS

Rapping poltergeists are comparatively common. A noisy haunting in Tennessee consisted of nothing but raps. Attempts were made to shoot the "ghost" and a door was struck open by a tremendous blow. Raps in connection with deaths are traditional and many times considered harbingers.

chapter   8

Visible Poltergeists

Visible Poltergeist Reported

The question of the visibility of the poltergeist is a
very complex problem and cannot be answered simply
and easily. The ghost proper, the apparition, is by common agreement visible, except in the case of the unseen
visitant whose presence is betrayed by footsteps, and
other traditional telltale actions. There is a vast body of
very well-known evidence substantiating the reality of
ghosts and apparitions. However, the nature of the apparition is still another problem. Probably, the majority
are obviously subjective in nature, but certain examples
give all indications of being "solid" and very objective.
G. N. M. Tyrrell, in his *Apparitions* for example, favored
the subjective theory, but certain evidence exists to the
contrary. In the case of the poltergeist—and I am making a very arbitrary distinction merely for the sake of
convenience at the moment—the question of visibility
does not yield a clear-cut answer.

As we have seen, it is difficult to draw a line dividing
ghosts from poltergeist-apparitions. Each has characteristics of the other, and their actions are in many ways
identical. Possibly, one difference lies in the sense of the
grotesque that so often accompanies poltergeist phenomena. Another way in which a poltergeist-haunting
differs from a "normal" haunting is that a person is
haunted rather than a place. Both, I fear are not reliable
distinctions and cannot be depended upon. In a gro-

tesque sense, we detect a remarkable similarity to the strange and fantastic effects reported in the phenomena of witchcraft.

Animal—and Other Forms

Probably, one of the very first things that one notices when reviewing the accounts of complex poltergeist disturbances is that many visible forms were reported, but unlike the more orthodox ghost, the visible forms were not necessarily limited to human shape. With the poltergeist, animal forms have been frequently reported.

This strange characteristic is also found in tales of animal familiars of witches, and even the names bestowed on poltergeist-entities were similar to the titles that familiars bore.

During the haunting, or poltergeist infestation of Epworth Rectory, several animal forms were seen by members of the Wesley family. A creature "like a white rabbit" was seen, and an animal "most like a badger" ran out from under a bed. Another visible being was seen, to judge from the statement, ". . . when soon after there came down the stairs behind her something like a man in a loose nightgown trailing after him."

During the Willington Mill poltergeist disturbance several visible beings were reported. A luminous, transparent figure in a window appearing as a priest in a white surplice was seen, and a young child said that she had seen a strange looking head of an old woman appear. Another child claimed that he had seen a "monkey," and reports of other apparitional forms were recorded.

Little visible phenomena was seen during the famous Drummer of Tedworth case which is really rather strange, considering that the disturbance offered violent effects of an extremely complex nature. A servant told of seeing a "great body with two red and glaring eyes," but was unable to describe its form. Unfortunately, this tale was not capable of being verified by other witnesses. Lights were seen, but they really fall into another classification and should not be included with visible apparitions.

It might be well to call attention to the fact again that certain of these apparitions, or forms, gave all indications of having possessed some characteristics of solid, normal matter. For example, sounds of ghostly garments disturbed by rapid motions have been noticed.

I use the term apparition to signify a visible being, or form, that may or may not have attributes of the normal, solid "orthodox," diaphanous ghost; the paranormal body of bilocation, or "astral projection"; the solid and normal appearing phantom; and lastly the strange animal forms reported in many poltergeist cases. Reported forms, real or not, such as the "great body with two red and glaring eyes" can also be included in this general classification.

In spite of the great diversity of phenomena encountered in the Ringcroft poltergeist-haunting, few visible forms were seen. On one occasion, however, a "little white Hand and an Arm, from the Elbow down," appeared which pushed the arm of a witness up. Testimony such as this supports the possibility of "solid" apparitional beings.

A fearsome "black thing" was seen in a corner of a barn and it seemed not to have any definite shape, but resembled a "black cloud." Again, the fantastic form apparently possessed certain material characteristics, for according to the witnesses it threw barley-chaff and mud at them, and also grasped them with great firmness and force.

With the Hinton Ampner poltergeist, however, phantasmic beings were seen. In July, 1776, a ghostly figure of a woman dressed in dark clothes was seen, and the phantom figure's dress rustled as it moved. A figure of a man in a dark colored suit was also seen.

A sinister note was struck when the infested house was finally pulled down. A small skull was found under the floor of a room, and it was said to have been that of a monkey. It was also claimed that rather than the skull of a monkey, it was that of a baby. No actual investigation was made, or perhaps was discouraged, and the true nature of the skull will always remain a mystery.

I found a quite curious little tale in a copy of the *Los Angeles Times* of 1956—I do not happen to have the day and month—which I include purely as an example of the traditional war ghost story. It has, of course, absolutely no evidential value whatsoever and undoubtedly is not factual in the least, but it is rather interesting as a typical tale that comes into being every so often, and is offered as a "collector's piece."

TOKYO, JULY 23RD (REUTERS)

The "ghosts" of Japanese soldiers who rise nightly to man a rusted anti-aircraft gun on the New Guinea beaches have so terrified the natives that they have asked a Japanese War Graves Commission to "appease" them.

The commission, touring New Guinea to collect the remains of Japanese soldiers killed there in World War II, said it was warned by the natives who claimed that every night the ghosts visit the rusting gun on the beaches of Hollandia.

During the heavy shelling by the United States Navy, April 5th, 1945, the gun was put out of commission and most of its crew killed.

The commission reported that when the war ended the natives began to whisper that "haggard soldiers in rusty helmets" arose to man the gun emplacements at midnight. Many terrified natives took off to visit relatives in distant places.

When the commission visited the area it was ap-

*proached by the natives and a Buddhist priest and
asked to perform a "purification ceremony" and "appease
the angry ghosts." The commission said that the rite will
be performed soon.*

Unfortunately, these traditional and popular tales do
not reflect fact. Psychical research, and the study of
poltergeist phenomena and hauntings in particular,
would have long ago been thoroughly recognized and
accepted by science if such predictable and periodic
ghosts did in fact exist!

As we have read, the Indian Poltergeist given in Fr.
Thurstion's collection, appeared as a dark, female figure that in answer to—"Who are you?" replied, "Why,
father." A written message was also found and was
signed, "Lourdes Mary," which was the name of the
deceased daughter.

If it had not been for the many other typical effects
of the poltergeist, one would be inclined to consider the
account more characteristic of haunting phenomena. A
spiritistic element was clearly shown by the phantom's
speech, and by the written message found on the wall,
which was said by the father to have closely resembled
that of his daughter.

Several examples of writing were discovered during
the case and all were found on the bathroom walls. This
curious preference certainly modifies any spiritualistic
interpretation that can be advanced, and is very typical
of the poltergeist, and, in fact, it can be suggested that
the apparition assumed to have been the dead daughter
was really a form taken by the poltergeist-force. Such
cases as these are indeed difficult to solve.

A Personal "Ghost" Actually Seen

I can offer only one phantasmic figure from my own experiences. It certainly was not spectacular compared to many other sightings, but a personal experience is always rewarding! As to which category it falls into I leave the decision to the reader. It did not resemble the "orthodox" ghost, or apparition, and it did not possess the attributes of the poltergeist.

The incident occurred in my home on February 5, 1955. I was seated on a couch in my bedroom leaning over tying my shoe laces when I saw something white flicker in front of me. I assumed it was my cat who was black and white, but I immediately noticed that she was lying on the far end of the couch. As I turned my head back I saw directly in front of me against a mahogany paneled wall a strange shadow. It was trapezoidal in form and was roughly the height of a man. It was "leaning" approximately twenty-five degrees to my right and had no visible contact with the floor. As I continued to stare in utter amazement, the shadow suddenly rushed through two open glass doors into the living room where it disappeared. The effect was as though a man had been standing in front of me and had suddenly wheeled about to move with incredible swiftness into the front room. I mechanically looked at the clock and noticed that it was 6:15 P.M.

The strange, trapezoidal form of the shadow offered a most remarkable coincidence—and I sincerely doubt that it was a coincidence—in that many years ago when I was about fourteen years of age, I had a most unpleasant nightmare that I have never been able to forget. At the beginning of the dream I saw a weird trapezoid of light pass across a wall several times and it heralded the later approach of a frightful spectre. The geometrical figure of light displayed the same inclination to the right as did the odd shadow. When I saw the shadow I immediately remembered my dream of years ago.

One of the poltergeist cases mentioned by Increase Mather in his *Remarkable Providences* included a reported phantom hand which some members of the family involved insisted they saw. They claimed, incidentally, that it threw the rocks that had fallen throughout the disturbance.

Ghostly Hands in Action

These ghostly hands that have been reported in several cases seem similar, if not identical, to the numerous paranormal hands that were seen during experimental seances with Eusapia Palladino. The hands witnessed in various poltergeist cases were, according to witnesses, quite capable of performing normal functions, as were the hands observed in the presence of the famous Italian medium. As is well-known, the many hands seen with Palladino appeared frequently over her head, and in other positions, and on numerous occasions held objects, touched sitters, and in general seemed very lifelike.

For example, during one of the American seances, a phantom hand reportedly lifted a photographic plate which was wrapped in several thicknesses of paper, and carried it into the seance-cabinet over a sitter's head.

Mr. Carrington, a pioneer psychist, described to me what he saw during a seance. In full light a small woman's hand reached up from under a table. He said that the hand had a lacy sleeve, but possessed no upper arm as though cut off at the wrist. There simply was nothing more and the hand was clearly visible for some time. The "little white hand and an Arm, from the Elbow down," which was seen during the Ringcroft infestation, certainly reminds us of the hand observed by Carrington.

It has been remarked that the very missiles thrown during poltergeist outbreaks give all indications of having been carried and tossed by invisible hands. Objects have actually poised themselves in the air before being hurled exactly as though an unseen hand and arm had raised and thrown them. Considering the observations, it must be admitted that evidence exists indicating that a mechanism for these motions can include invisible hands. Of course, it is not suggested that such an "explanation" covers all types of motions of objects—far from that!

During the seances with Eusapia Palladino many investigators were tapped, pinched, grasped, and struck by unseen hands, and on occasion, actual fingers were felt, offering a direct parallel to the invisible hands that may have acted in some manifestations of the poltergeist.

CHAPTER HIGHLIGHTS

Visible poltergeists have been seen. Hauntings and poltergeists are very similar. The nature of poltergeist-apparitions is very complex. Animal and non-human forms have often been reported. An apparition was personally seen by the author as a shadowy, geometrical form. Phantom hands have been frequently seen, and possibly can propel objects such as rocks.

chapter 9

Talking Poltergeists

Ghostly Voices Reported

Vocal poltergeists and ghosts have been heard and chronicled over the years. We have descriptions of sounds attributed to these paranormal beings, and they cover a most remarkable range. Yells, screams, bellows, whistlings, whispers, laughs, sobs, grunts, and every imaginable sound possible have been heard at one time or another. Though fantastic to read, splendidly reported cases have presented evidence of a very high order telling us of these voices.

Fraudulent Seances and Fraudulent Voices

Popular spiritualistic literature is filled with glowing accounts of spontaneous happenings and stories from the professional seance room enumerating marvel after marvel, each one more unbelievable than its predecessor. Voices are heard speaking through trumpets, emanating from materializations, and phantoms of all descriptions, and even from the empty air itself. Voices speak, shout and whisper single words, whole sentences, and entire glib sermons. I have sat hour upon hour listening to these vocal marvels—all the product of utter and complete fraud! Some "spirits" possessed vocabularies of reasonable extent and others surely originated from near-illiterates. At times, I have been amused, but usually bored, and on numerous occasions revolted and disgusted. The appalling thing is not the fraud and duplicity of the medium (*that* can be expected), or the ruthless, callous greed that is so many times displayed, but the gullibility of the spectators and believers.

It seems that no matter how inconceivably crude or childish the fakery may be, there are always followers who are willing to swallow the ridiculous performances whole. One would think that the very content of the messages alone would give rise to suspicion, but no matter how foolish the speech, the medium's circle is always eager and happy to accept all without the slightest doubt.

The "physical phenomena" that accompany the "voices" are of equal quality. The materializations are obviously the medium dressed in a "spook suit," or, at times, merely cloth waved about, sometimes on the end of a stick. The "spirit lights" that occasionally manifest with the materializations originate from a small flashlight with a pin-hole opening, and frequently a clumsy medium can be seen moving against accidental light-leaks producing telekinetic performances, raps, and the like.

Woe be to him who attempts to point out to a believer the fact that all is not necessarily what it may seem. The doubting Thomas is a most deep-dyed villain indeed, for there is nothing more vile and blasphemous than an investigator. Double damned be he who admits to skepticism about a point or two.

A Talking Poltergeist in Spain

Probably the best known case of a talking ghost, or poltergeist, is that of the Saragossa Ghost.

It was first published in *Historic Poltergeists* by Carrington and Fodor, Bulletin of the International Institute for Psychical Research, and the American Psychical Institute, 1935.

The incident took place in 1934 and was the subject of several newspaper accounts. One told of the ghost, or poltergeist, and its bizarre habit of speaking down a chimney pipe. The article went on to say that some workmen and an architect were asked to investigate the house and the mystery.

The chimney, or flue, served a number of apartments in the building and the voice that was heard came out of the pipe which was directly over the stove. The "ghost" spoke to tenants who lived in the building, and according to reports, also spoke to the police investigating the case, and called them by name. The newspaper reported that the voice spoke continuously.

The family and the young girl involved were removed for a night. The police waited for the voice, but nothing happened. As we know, this is exactly what could have been expected, for with the removal of the girl (the poltergeist-medium), no phenomena could take place. The police withdrew from the case having found nothing unusual, and nothing illegal.

The girl was examined by "medical experts" and a neurologist said that he believed that she was either a ventriloquist, or that someone was using a trick device.

Finally the Civil Governor of Saragossa, a city in Spain, on December 4th, declared that the mystery was solved, and the girl was an "unconscious" ventriloquist. Here the mystery of the talking ghost officially ended.

Although the case has been described in several works devoted to poltergeist phenomena, due to its remarkable nature and the fact that it was the subject of such widespread publicity I felt that it should at least be briefly described.

A "Talking" Mongoose

A very entertaining, controversial and dubious case is that of Gef, the Talking Mongoose. A major part of the phenomena, which supposedly happened, consisted of the voice of Gef. As is well-known, the mongoose presumably was an intelligent little creature who developed the ability to talk.

A number of investigators studied the case and most came to a negative conclusion. One investigator studied the mystery and finally decided that the case was not authentic.

Haunting of a Saint

Saint John Baptist Vianney, during the winter of 1824-25, at the age of thirty-eight, became the victim of a particularly malicious poltergeist persecution. Typical movements of objects occurred over an extended period of time. The curtains of his bed were shredded at night. Knockings were frequently heard, and voices occasionally spoke. On one occasion the mysterious voice shouted, *Vianney, Vianney! Potato eater! Ah, you are not yet dead? I will get you yet!*

Naturally, these grotesque phenomena were believed to have been a manifestation of the devil. It must be admitted that without stretching a point, the nature of the poltergeist at times has presented a thoroughly evil and diabolic aspect. It is difficult to see how at an earlier period such phenomena could have been taken for anything but a product of hellish intervention.

More Talking Poltergeists

During the complex and violent poltergeist-haunting at ancient Ringcroft a number of paranormal voices were reported. When the family was at prayers the poltergeist cried, *Hush! hush!* and at other times during prayers it whistled and groaned. These ghostly interruptions were, as we have so often seen, merely one of the many types of manifestations aimed at disrupting religious activity. The prevailing spirit of the invading force was malignant and clearly anti-religious.

Vocal efforts of the poltergeist resulted in more whistles and groans, and the curious words, "Bo, Bo Cuck," were heard again at prayers. While these strange words were voiced various witnesses were pulled about and mud was thrown into their faces. Other attempts at interference with religious activities involved the throwing of stones while prayers were said.

On one occasion the mysterious voice called the occupants of the besieged house, "Witches" and "Rooks," and said that it would take them to hell. After this pleasantry the voice added, *Thou shalt not be troubled till Tuesday.*

During the typical but rather mild manifestations that disturbed the Wesley family at Epworth, the poltergeist confined itself primarily to knockings and poundings. A few sound effects were heard, however, and included deep groans, a gobbling sound, and other vocal efforts. As we have mentioned, other activities encountered by the Wesleys were animal forms reminiscent of the animal familiars of the witches.

In the chapter entitled "An Indian Poltergeist" from Fr. Herbert Thurston's *Ghosts and Poltergeists,* a most amazing case is described which includes varied and violent effects of advanced order. The usual dislike for religion was displayed, but it seemed to be aimed at the Christianity of the converted Hindu family who suffered the visitation of the malevolent force, rather than at religion in general.

Apparently, two words only were spoken by the phantasmic invader, and they were spoken by an apparition. The words said, "Why, father," plainly implied that the figure was the spirit of a dead daughter, and with these words, a spiritualistic element entered the case.

The phenomena manifested an extreme ferocity and malignance, and a general similarity to the phenomena of possession and witchcraft was displayed. As we have mentioned, the hatred for matters religious was very prominent.

An example rivaling the Saragossa Ghost was reported by Dr. Encausse. In Valence-en-Brie, France, a small village of 700 inhabitants, a troubled house existed, and more than fifty witnesses testified in court to the reality of the phenomena seen in this house and one other.

The first phenomenon noticed was a loud, gruff voice using coarse language, and was first heard by a maid in a cellar. A dozen neighbors verified the incident. Later, the voice encompassed the entire house in its field of activity. The voice seemed to emanate from the ground, and it was stated that it originated from so many sources that trickery seemed impossible.

Other paranormal effects occurred including the spontaneous shattering of window panes in daylight in full view of the tenants. Furniture was moved about in an unoccupied room, and general telekinetic (the movement of objects without normal contact) phenomena took place throughout the house.

The manifestations were supposedly traced to an invalid tenant who moved to another house to escape the poltergeist, but to her dismay the ghostly invader followed her there. Dr. Encausse believed, however, that the uncanny events were centered about a young servant girl.

Many other cases exist during which paranormal voices were encountered, but the few examples given in this chapter represent typical occurrences.

CHAPTER HIGHLIGHTS

Mysterious and untraceable voices have been heard, but fraudulent voices are common in "professional" seances. The paranormal persecution of St. Vianney is described and other speaking poltergeists briefly described but no conventional explanation of the phenomena has been shown to date.

chapter 10

Watery Poltergeists

Mysterious Influxes of Water

A rather rare effect found with the poltergeist is the mysterious appearance of water. The amount of liquid may consist of a few drops, or a near-deluge. Several cases including watery phenomena are found in the works of Charles Fort.

A booklet entitled *The Snettisham Ghost* by Rev. Rowland W. Maitland offers a remarkable study of a haunting and the appearance of apparitions and is an extension of a case published in the *Proceedings* of the Society for Psychical Research. Included is a brief statement in an account by a Dr. Marshall which describes the haunting. Noises had been heard in a house for several years and a Miss Ackland on one occasion was in the attic kneeling by a trunk when water was sprinkled at her. After this incident she found that the nearby wall had been wetted and a small puddle of water was on the floor.

A case published in the *Annals of Psychic Science*, April, 1906, described a poltergeist-disturbed house that offered the usual displacement of furniture, tinkling of small bells, and abnormal sprinklings of water.

Charles Fort mentioned in his *Lo!* that he had records of about sixty cases involving appearances of water and other phenomena. The well-known Eccleston, England, case that occurred in 1873 is given by Fort as well as the remarkable appearance of various liquids including showers of water that took place at Swanton Novers Rectory, England, 1919. At that time it was reported that about fifty gallons of oil had been caught from the poltergeist phenomena. A confession was featured, but it undoubtedly had little bearing on the reality of the phenomena. The famous Wellesley, Ontario, Canada, case of 1880 is also given in *Lo!* and furnishes reports of falls of water inside an old house.

Fr. Thurston gives an example in his *Ghosts and Poltergeists* which describes the phenomena observed by Prof. Dorfler with the poltergeist-medium, Frieda Weissal. The usual telekinetic flights of objects were seen and people were slightly wetted with water, including the medium.

A Watery Poltergeist in Massachusetts

Other such cases have existed, but we now refer to a very recent and remarkable case; the mysterious appearance of water at Lawrence and Methuen, Mass. Here are excerpts from the first notice that appeared in a Lawrence paper on Nov. 2, 1963.

Water from an unexplainable source is practically chasing a local family of Methuen around the city.

Last Tuesday the family noticed a wet spot on the wall of their TV room. A few moments later they heard a pop, like a firecracker and water squirted from the wall. This continued until Friday when there was so much moisture in the house that the family had to abandon it for a night and move to the home of a relative. Saturday morning the weird events began all over again.

Five people have seen the strange phenomena. . . .

A crew of city firemen, two of them with extensive building experience, were assigned to check the roof for leaks and crawl space between the dutch flat on the third floor and the roof.

The men report the roof is sound. There is no sign of moisture or leaks in the crawl space and lights flashed down partitions from the roof fail to reveal a trace of water.

Neither the first floor or third floor apartments are having any trouble, only the apartment of Mr. & Mrs. A.

The Fire Deputy verifies the fact that every squirt from the wall is preceded by a popping noise. He said that there is no hole in the wall afterward . . .

Firemen also verified that there were no pipes leaking and eliminated that as a source of the water.

But, weird as things were Saturday at the A's apartment, things were even worse at another residence in Methuen.

A representative at a local roofing company called in to test a home in Methuen reports, "There was a quart of water on the sofa. I reached up and pulled down the plaster board and it was as dry as a bone." He says that he has never seen anything like it before.

The owner claims the humidity in his house rose from a normal 38 to 40 all the way to 68 and then things really began to pop.

*He said they tried everything possible to explain
the situation.*

*"They shut off the water and drained the pipes. They
shut off the heat and opened windows. They raised all
the shades to let in as much sunlight as possible. Nothing seemed to help."*

*. . . contended that this moisture builds up and that
the weather since Saturday when it was hot, and Monday when it was cold, produced the right circumstances
to cause the fountains in the walls.*

*This, the owner believes, is possible for his house, but
what explanation is there to offer for the apartment?*

*If the accumulation of condensation is to blame there,
too, why is it not spouting leaks in the first and third
floor also? (A very significant question indeed.)*

The next issue to describe the strange events plaguing
the family was published Nov. 4, 1963, and furnished
several theories presumably explaining the mystery. I
will give a condensed version of the article and a few
direct quotations.

It was stated that on Saturday no explanations would
suffice, but "Now there are enough explanations so you
can take your pick."

"The case of the water-squirting walls is officially
closed so far as the family, Lawrence police, and the
Lawrence and Methuen fire departments are concerned.
However, each has its own explanation."

Again, the very significant observation was made that,
"the tenant occupies the middle floor of a three-tenant
dwelling. The squirting walls were confined to the one
apartment."

Further: "In a report from the police station, investigating officers said that a daughter admitted throwing
water on the walls of her grandmother's apartment
with a water glass. As far as the police are concerned
the matter is closed."

However, the officials from the Methuen and Lawrence fire departments did not agree with the police theory—or explanation. For instance, the Deputy Chief of Methuen remarked that the girl was helping to "mop up the house when water was exploding in four or five places at once."

"Neither the grandmother nor the parents agree with the police. They claim the girl admitted spilling the water in the pantry and breaking a glass."

After reading these somewhat confused but typical articles I wrote to an investigating expert asking for further information. He kindly replied and a condensed version follows:

This particular condition started during the first part of the week in the home of Mr. and Mrs. Y and daughter, aged eleven, at their home in Methuen, Mass, which is about three miles from here. According to them the condition gradually became worse; so much so that by Friday evening they could no longer occupy the house. The wife went to a girl friend's house for the night and the husband and his daughter came down to Lawrence and stayed with the wife's mother who lived in an apartment.

During the week the Y's had an engineer out of Boston who represented one of the more prominent roofing manufacturers. . . . He stayed in the area all week and worked along with the Y's and the Methuen Fire Department to help solve the mystery. There was water everywhere. Mrs. Y and her relatives worked on the three floors of their cottage mopping up water and attempting to dry out the place with dehumidifying apparatus. There, the fire department went so far as to pull down plaster walls only to find that the wall from which the water came was perfectly dry.

This expert described the investigation which included

over seven men and concluded that there was nothing whatsoever wrong with the building structurally. In the next paragraphs of his letter he mentions an incident which can be so very typical in poltergeist cases, and which can prove a formidable stumbling block to the layman and a great nuisance to the researcher.

At one time I was standing in such a position in the kitchen that I also had the pantry wall in my vision. The eleven year old girl was in the pantry at the time, but obscured from my vision. I heard her yell, "There's the water again," and I quickly took in the pantry wall, and what I saw was water either leaving the wall, or bouncing off the wall. . . .

At this time there were twelve adults in the five room apartment. There were nine from the fire department, the landlord, Mr. Y and his mother-in-law. This water condition was happening in every room in the apartment.

The police heard about it at the same time and came up. At one time while they were there the daughter went into the pantry for a drink of water. One of the police officers followed her. When she turned and saw him she dropped the glass. The officer asked her if she had water in the glass and she said no. I learned later that she did have water in the glass, but said no because she could see the implication. After further questioning she admitted she did have water in the glass for a drink.

The police then and there wrote off their part of the investigation with the notation that whatever damage had been done was done by the daughter. We knew this could not be so because, for one thing she could not have got away with it with twelve adults in the house, and further, it was happening in Methuen.

The expert remarked that the Methuen Fire Department disagreed with the Lawrence police theory on the basis of what they had observed there, and added a paragraph which contains several interesting and important observations.

Mrs. Y said that one time she had five relatives mopping up water in Methuen while the eleven year old was with her grandmother in Lawrence. We wrote it off as a bad experience, and to speak to any of the men who did observe the condition would only cause them to shake their heads and wonder what they actually did see. It had become so mystifying in Methuen that traffic jams were being caused by the curious. People would go up to the Y's and touch their clothes with the thought that some spiritual help would be theirs. To avoid this concern which was now becoming ridiculous in Methuen, the Y's announced that a hole had been found in their roof which accounted for the water. The public accepted it and the whole thing just died away. I contacted the Methuen Fire Department and they told me why the Y's had made the statement. This still did not explain the situation in Lawrence.

I again wrote to the expert asking him "formally" if he thought that the child could have possibly aided, or caused the water effects fradulently, and if he considered the appearance of the water an abnormal phenomenon.

He replied that he considered "the appearance of the water abnormal for both Lawrence and Methuen." He further stated, fraud had not been present. "Firstly, because it seems almost impossible for the girl to do that (tossing water about in the large amounts necessary to equal the phenomena) with so many people in the house, as I explained to you. Again, there is her grandmother's testimony that water appeared in the living room before the girl got out of bed that morning."

It was further added that, "If there was any fakery in

this matter, I have not been made aware of it. From our observations at the time we did not see anything that would indicate fakery."

I also contacted the Methuen Fire Department and a statement was sent remarking that water had been held in the insulation of the Y's home and when conditions were exactly right, the water was released inside the house. The water had gained entrance by means of a previously undiscovered hole in the roof.

In another letter the expert clarified the apparent contradictions created by the Methuen department's statement and wrote:

As for (the Methuen Fire Department) I believe I told you that they told me that they were giving out a story that they felt would end the incident. One of the national roofing concerns was interested and they had an engineer out of Boston go to the Methuen address and stay in the area for a few days. He came up with nothing as far as roof leaks, insulation, etc., and the building was given a thorough examination. As for the insulation, it could not possibly hold the water. It could get damp, or even wet, and when it did the water would follow the forces of gravity and find its way out at the bottom. Further, if there had been a previously undiscovered hole in the roof, and it did admit water, the wetting or dampness, would only be in the immediate, or general area, and not in all parts of the house.

In the Lawrence case there was no insulation in the building, and as I have told you, the apartment is a second floor apartment in a three story building, and there was no moisture of any kind on the third floor . . .

I discussed the case extensively via letters with Rev. Guy J. Cyr, S.M. of the Sacred Heart Rectory in Lawrence who had investigated the incident. He had talked to the Y's, and, of course, was very familiar with the entire affair, and did not believe that fraud had entered into the picture. Rev. Cyr kindly sent me a very interesting paper dealing with watery phenomena which contained numerous interesting and valuable observations, and I include a number of them. . . .

I am fully aware of the fact that there was an awful lot of water; one witness said that at one time he actually saw it cascading down the staircase. In one room several testified that there was at least one inch of it on the floor. A few times, according to reports, as much as a quart of it would splash at once. But there were many people there. Once there were as many as twenty-five.

Note here Mr. Y's own words: "First, there is a noise like a firecracker, then the water shoots out."

. . . that, at least according to some witnesses, on Saturday, Nov. 1st, water was bubbling and/or "shooting" on the walls and furniture of five rooms "at the same time" in Mrs. Y's mother's apartment. . . .

. . . I have to mention a few yet unpublished facts reported by the witnesses: Just before each explosion a hissing noise was heard, lasting for about a second and sounding like a burning, powdered fuse, just before the firecracker explodes. Then came the explosion described variously as something like the snapping of the thumb against one of the fingers, or like a firecracker, or a toy cricket. Then, or immediately after, the water was seen (and heard?) to squirt on the wall, and in a most peculiar way. The jets of water would arch up to one side, making semi-circles on, or near, the wall. It was noticed that invariably that spot on the wall felt unexplainably warm, or hot, and that the wet spot dried up in a very short time. That is important, considering that the air was already loaded, almost saturated with moisture. As soon as it was completely dry, or nearly so, another explosion occurred on the same spot, and in the same way, except that the semi-circular streams of water went in a

*direction opposite to that of the first. After a while the
spectators got on to the rhythm of the two explosions.
Another type of rhythmic action was mentioned. When
the witnesses had seen an explosion on one wall, they
would expect another on another wall. And they were
not disappointed. Were they unconsciously a part of it
at least in part? . . . A third rhythmic event: When a
few bubbles were noticed on furniture, the spectators
would talk as if they expected more, and their predic-
tions were fulfilled in a few moments. Whether or not
the tempos of these various rhythms were calculated
exactly, I don't know yet. Also the bubbles on the furniture were at times as big "as marbles."*

A rather humorous aspect of the case was encountered during an interview with Mrs. Y. A somewhat
widely known self-styled researcher on TV discussed
the case with her, but prior to the broadcast managed to
antagonize her by suggesting that her daughter was
the cause of the phenomena due to extreme piety. Mrs.
Y, I understand, very appropriately retorted that if piety
were the cause some would be wet most of the time.
She further remarked that her daughter was the usual
type and certainly had displayed no unusual devotional
attitudes.

The investigator then suggested through a long and
curious chain of "logic" that perhaps certain woods
included in the afflicted house had been associated in
a quite fantastic way with an Indian, and his ghost was
protesting by means of the strange water manifestations!
Mrs. Y then refused to go on the air if such nonsense
was going to be discussed. Consequently, the resulting
interview was most sedate and conservative.

Rev. Cyr sent me another letter remarking that the
authorities in Methuen "gave a solution to the mystery
knowing all the time that it was no solution at all so that
the curious would not bother Mr. & Mrs. Y any more."

Speaking of the interview mentioned which took place Feb. 28th, 1964, several very interesting observations were made by Mrs. Y. She said, for example, that on Oct. 25 four members of the household, including her daughter and herself all witnessed the squirting water above the television. She said that the water arched out into the room, and lasted for over two hours. Fraud by her daughter is clearly ruled out in ths case. She also kept referring to the fact that the jetting water later came from all parts of the house and with explosive noises.

Case Review

In general *it can be said that paranormal phenomena did occur.* The police report that the Y's daughter admitted throwing water, does not, to my mind, alter the main elements of the case. Perhaps later in the course of the disturbance water had been introduced normally, but this does not alter earlier observations of witnesses concerning phenomena which obviously occurred under good conditions. Again, it must be remembered that the case is not merely one isolated example of the mysterious appearance of water, but is one of a number of its kind!

CHAPTER HIGHLIGHTS

Unexplainable influxes of water poltergeists have occurred. In a recent and remarkable case in Massachusetts, water jetted from walls accompanied by explosive sounds. An expert stated that the phenomena observed was certainly of abnormal origin. In spite of voluminous conventional evidence, it could not be proved that the water poltergeist was other than paranormal in its source.

chapter 11

Poltergeist Incendiaries and Arsonists

Fires and Hauntings Associated

Fire, as with small children, seems to be a favorite plaything of the poltergeist. In practically all of the very complex, major cases, unaccountable fires have been present in one form or another. The Ringcroft poltergeist set furniture ablaze; set the house afire twenty-seven times during one day, threw a large quantity of burning peat inside the besieged house, threw a hot stone into the children's bed between the children and burned through the bedding, brought bundles of burning straw into the yard, and created an effect of "fire-balls" falling inside the house. It was said that the fire vanished as the fire-balls fell.

Typical Examples

In the case of the Haunted House of La Constantinie reported by Professor Flammarion, thick smoke was found issuing from a bed and smoke was also seen coming from the skirts of an elderly lady living there.

The Drummer of Tedworth poltergeist, during its vicious persecution of the children of the house, threw lighted candles under their bed. Its incendiary activities, however, seem to have been rather limited.

An account of a series of mysterious fires was printed

in the *St. Louis Globe-Democrat*, December 19th, 1891, which described a series of blazes that spontaneously occurred in the presence of a fourteen year old girl.

The *Los Angeles Times*, April 4th, 1960, contained an interesting account of a fiery poltergeist which I quote essentially as follows:

GEORGETOWN, BRITISH GUIANA, APRIL 3, 1960.

A newspaper reporter tore the shirt off 15 year old Carl Lopes yesterday when it mysteriously caught fire.

That made the sixth unexplained blaze of the day in the house of John Lopes where, the story is, dozens of fires have broken out for no apparent reason over the last three weeks. The Lopes family of 11 is near distraction as a result of the flames, which have left the police and fire departments baffled.

Thursday night, after four blazes which destroyed or damaged articles in the house, a group from the Salvation Army came and offered prayers. Yesterday the fires continued. A book entitled The Preachings of Jesus Christ was among the articles burned. Carl's shirt caught fire in the presence of Daily Chronicle reporter Trenton Paul. Lopes had just finished showing Paul how the tail of the shirt had been scorched in an earlier fire when it suddenly broke out into flames.

Paul said several other persons were in the house at the time, but, "no one was close enough to have had any connection with the fire."

A seamstress visited the family yesterday to sympathize. She took along some dress material belonging to a client. Suddenly it caught fire and before she could beat out the flames, the cloth was a charred ruin.

The tale is so very typical of the fire-poltergeist that it can almost be considered a classic example. The presence of a child, the fifteen year old Lopes, could well have supplied the focal point of the poltergeist-force, as is found in most cases. The mysterious appearance of the fires and the destruction of a religious article, the book, all are characteristic actions. It is not, of course, possible to arrive at any conclusive judgment regarding the case, inasmuch as the only information available consists of a very short newspaper article. The recorded events, though, fit so well into the pattern of the poltergeist that the probabilities strongly suggest the reality and genuineness of the phenomena.

A Case in Texas

The *Houston Post*, April 25, 1964, included a short article describing a typical disturbance of apparent poltergeist origin that happened at the home of Mr. and Mrs. J. According to the news report chairs were hurled here and there, various kitchen pieces were thrown about, and in one room several fires of mysterious nature burst out. I wrote requesting more information and Mrs. J. replied, giving a few more details of the odd incident. Unfortunately I was not able to contact her again and consequently more information including the actual date of the happening was not obtainable. In spite of the scarcity of detail and verification the case is quite interesting in general, and the fires in particular.

Mrs. J. remarked that about 12:30, while she and her husband were in the dining room, a curtain suddenly began to blaze. The curtain was quickly torn from the window and the fire put out when another first burst into flame "about three inches above the door, burnt through the wallpaper, and went out." The damaged area was about two inches wide and ten inches long. "About five minutes later another fire broke out about the same size and it went out." Other blazes occurred totalling about nine fires.

A fire inspector was called but obviously was at a loss to explain the strange phenomenon. He advised that the wall paper be pulled from the walls, which was done, and suggested that he be called in case of more fires.

Later, a number of chairs fell down; a flower vase, a water glass, and a sugar bowl, were "turning over," and other objects were also displaced. Again, the typical tricks of the poltergeist were displayed.

Quite frequently cases are reported in such a manner that it is very obvious that the reporter and those involved have simply never heard of poltergeist phenomena, and in fact, are not familiar with the word poltergeist. This became very noticeable to me while investigating the Big Bear City rockfall. The witnesses I talked to were completely unaware of such a paranormal force, and really believed that the phenomenon they had seen was unique, and had never happened before.

This factor, of course, greatly aids in an investigation. When a witness is plainly unaware of both terms and subject, and his description of phenomena matches the pattern of other authentic examples, then the truth of his statements becomes highly probable and evident. A person not familiar with the descriptions and theories of poltergeist activity will have some difficulty inventing proper detail and may well give himself away. To be more exact, I have been told many a tale of hauntings and poltergeist infestation where incorrect detail and faulty pattern revealed a hoax.

Both the Lopes case and the preceding incident have all the earmarks of authenticity. The descriptions, though limited, certainly indicate the existence of genuine paranormal forces.

The well-known Great Amherst Mystery offered extremely violent and unusual phenomena and fantastic fires of weird origin played a very significant part. According to the book by Walter Hubbell odd fires were manifested on several occasions. Lighted matches fell from the ceiling onto a bed and would have set it afire if they had not been quickly extinguished. On one occasion a dress was taken from a nail in the wall, rolled up, placed under a bed and set aflame. Again, the fire was put out before damage occurred. Shavings in the cellar were found ablaze and in turn were put out before serious damage occurred. A barn belonging to a neighbor was burned down after Esther Cox, the poltergeist-medium, had gone to his house to live.

Unfortunately, the shadow of suspicion clouds this case which is fascinating in certain aspects. Dr. Walter Franklin Prince discussed the case in Volume XIII of the *Proceedings* of the American Society for Psychical Research and viewed it in a very unfavorable light. He considered that nearly all the effects reported were fradulent, but I must admit that some of his arguments seem too extreme.

Harry Price stated that he thought the case was well authenticated and that the phenomena had been witnessed by a number of reputable persons including medical men. Hereward Carrington considered the case at the very least genuine in part; all of which shows that the various authorities have been unable to agree on this strange and truly grotesque example.

The Phelps Case

A very remarkable and startling infestation occurred in 1850-1851 and has been entitled the Phelps Case. Extraordinary phenomena were encountered, including a fantastic tableau consisting of eleven figures, all female but one, constructed of clothing which had been gathered from various parts of the afflicted house. The figures were arranged in devotional attitudes and a number of Bibles were before them, opened at appropriate passages related to paranormal activities that had happened. The passages were described as favorable to the phenomena. Mysterious fires were found during the progress of this case.

More Fires and Poltergeists

A similar case was given in the *New York Herald,* January 6th, 1895, which told of a fire-beleaguered home that was ultimately destroyed. Both police and firemen who were present were baffled, and the Fire Marshal said, . . . *I have no explanation to offer as to the cause of the fire, or the throwing around of the furniture.* The bedeviled family eventually lost everything but their clothes. From the moment that the first fire burst into flame until twenty hours later when the house was destroyed, fires were seen frequently in places where they could not have possibly been started normally, according to witnesses.

The *New York World,* August 8th, 1887, reported a fiery poltergeist that burned a frame house which was occupied by a man and wife, four children and two nieces. About forty fires were discovered within a few hours that could not be traced to a human agency.

On January 10th, 1958, a series of strange fires plagued a home in Montana. Curtains were destroyed, a portable wardrobe with clothes inside was burned, a fire was found in a dresser, and other objects were set ablaze. No normal explanation seemed adequate to solve the mystery.

The fascinating case, *An Indian Poltergeist,* included in Father Thurston's *Ghosts and Poltergeists,* displayed fire-phenomena on numerous occasions. Clothes were set afire, extinguished with water, and again found burning. The chair that they had been placed upon was also aflame. Particular hatred was shown for anything of a religious nature. Pictures of the Virgin, saints, and the like were set afire, and a crucifix was tossed into a fire. Wood from the hearth was thrown about while burning and a thatched shed was set ablaze, but the fire was put out before it was destroyed. There seems little doubt that the poltergeist had actually attempted to completely destroy the house, and probably the occupants if the opportunity had been there.

It has been suggested that during these odd, fiery cases, the poltergeist-force actually did not attempt to burn house and occupants, but in reality fully intended to have the fires found before serious damage was done. Perhaps this was true in certain examples, but considering the cases concerning ruined homes, burned possessions and obvious attempts at destruction and death, I see little reason to doubt that the poltergeist's intentions were completely malign and murderous.

As suggested, the poltergeist seemingly presents a dual nature. In certain examples fires were set in places that were bound to have been discovered. In these cases the poltergeist appeared to have had a protective aspect.

A Case In Canada

The dual nature was exemplified in an extremely active and complex case that began September 15th, 1889, and troubled the family of a farmer in the township of Clarendon, Province of Quebec. Reported violent phenomena included a gruff voice that spoke frequently. One interesting conversation consisted of the voice informing the family that, *I am the devil*. A following statement claimed that "he" would have them in his clutches, and not to interfere lest they suffer a broken neck.

After one attempt to set the house afire the owner asked the "devil" why he had been persecuting his family. The voice answered that it was continuing the maliciousness just for the fun of it! The farmer replied that he thought it was not humorous to have thrown a stone and hit "little Mary." The voice remarked that it had been an accident, and in spite of the girl having been struck, she was at least prevented from being injured. The question was also asked why had the house been set on fire and the poltergeist said that the fires had always been started in the daytime, and expressed sorrow over their occurrence.

The human-like qualities of the invading force are very evident here and the motives mixed. Inasmuch as the language of the poltergeist had not been noted for its purity and good-will, a visitor remarked on the fact that the communications had generally improved. A rather grandiloquent reply informed all that "he" was not the one who had been prone to using coarse language, but instead was an angel from heaven sent to drive away the offender. However, as we read on, we find that the heavenly tenor was of short duration. As the questioning continued the voice became confused, lost its temper, and lapsed back into not so heavenly speech.

CHAPTER HIGHLIGHTS

Mysterious fires occur during poltergeist infestations. Numerous fires plagued a boy in British Guiana and a religious service or exorcism proved ineffectual. A home in Texas became the scene of repeated fires and other violent phenomena. A complex case in Canada offered extremely violent effects, including several fires, and a very human-like voice of the invading poltergeist was clearly heard.

chapter 12

Human Combustion

Humans Consumed by Fire

One of the strangest effects that has on occasion been attributed to the poltergeist is the grim and grotesque phenomenon of human combustion. There have been reported poltergeist cases where extreme property damage resulted, and cases where families in poor circumstances were burned out of their homes and left destitute. There has been an account of a case where the victims of the attentions of a poltergeist, two children, were so terrified by the strange phenomena that took place in their home that one, a girl, died apparently through the effects of fear. The other, a boy, was taken to a hospital with a nervous breakdown.

There has even been a case reported by Fort where the visitations of a poltergeist resulted in smashed windows and thrown crockery, and so frightened the members of a family that a daughter broke down with fright, a granddaughter went insane, a son was taken to an institution after smashing furniture in a wild fit, and the mother ran in panic from the house into a forest where she hid for three days wild with terror. These stories are cheerless, but even more grim are the mysterious deaths caused by self-combustion that have occasionally been reported.

The subject is complex, puzzling, and difficult to categorize. Some have seriously suggested that these grotesque cases are the result of what can best be described as poltergeist-attack. Before we attempt to classify and explain, however, a number of examples will be given, and a brief description of the effects assayed.

For reasons that at the present are unknown, a living human body can literally burst into flames and be almost entirely consumed by an incredible heat. Frequently, surroundings such as furniture, curtains, walls, and even clothes worn by the victim may be left comparatively untouched by the strange flames. On other occasions the nearby surroundings are normally consumed by the fires. Many times these blazes show eccentricities of behavior that appear extremely abnormal. It has been noticed, for example, that in some cases the victims did not seem aware that they were actually in flames, and apparently felt no pain. At other times the very opposite was true.

A typical and recent example of this fiery phenomena was described in the *Boston Sunday Globe*, December 9th, 1956. It was reported that an invalid widow, Mrs. C., 78, was burned to death in a mysterious blaze that was limited to her kitchen rocking chair. Her daughter informed the police that her mother was not a smoker, and that the fire could not have been attributed to cigarettes. The daughter lived at the same address. The fire department was not able to determine the source of the mysterious fire.

The Fiery Death of Mrs. Reeser

On a morning in July, 1951, the doorknob to Mrs. Reeser's room was discovered by her landlady to be mysteriously hot to the touch. Some workmen were called and after they had forcibly opened the door they were appalled at the terrible and incredible sight that met their eyes.

Little that was recognizable was left of the occupant. Mrs. Reeser, a woman of one hundred and seventy pounds, had almost entirely been consumed by flames of unknown origin and the residue left consisted of her skull, fantastically shrunken in size, her left foot, and a number of seared vertabrae.

Her shrunken skull compounded an already incredible mystery for it is known that the human head undergoing extraordinary heat does not shrink upon itself but actually explodes or swells to great size.

It is also known that bodies burning in fires of 2,000°F., even for periods of eight hours, still retain a majority of recognizable bones identifiable as human in origin. It requires temperatures of over 3,000°F. to melt or volatilize bone. Professor Milton M. Krogman of the University of Pennsylvania Graduate School of Medicine who investigated this bizarre puzzle and is an expert upon this unusual and grim subject, noted these facts and related them to the Reeser case.

Evidence of the fierce flames which had destroyed Mrs. Reeser was found in the fact that the walls of her room were blackened by a greasy deposit of soot. The chair in which she had been sitting was almost totally burned, a mirror on a wall cracked by the tremendous heat of the blaze, and many other indications of the fierce fire were evident.

The police in what was perhaps an act of desperation, attributed Mrs. Reeser's cremation to a fire caused by a cigarette. It was also stated that the flames fed upon the victim's body fat. Needless to say, this explanation simply does not cover the facts, and in particular, cannot explain the incredible heat necessary to have consumed and even volatilized bone.

Naturally, various possible causes for the fire were carefully examined. Lightning was easily eliminated. The remaining ashes and residue were analyzed and it was determined that chemicals or fluids that could have started the blaze, or add to it, were not present. It was again noted that many hours of burning at extraordinary heat—2,500° to 3,000° F.—were demanded, and all investigation simply added mystery to mystery.

As an interesting and unusual literary aside to this strange and bizarre subject, a case of spontaneous combustion was described in *Bleak House* by Charles Dickens. However, it is not so well known that Emile Zola used the same "device" to remove a character in one of his novels.

An alcoholic peasant was consumed leaving only a residue of ashes. According to Zola, he had been resting in front of a fire, had fallen asleep, and dropped his pipe upon himself. A small blaze resulted and soon his destruction by fire took place.

At the moment I cannot recall the use of human combustion in other works of fiction although I have heard that an American novel has employed this phenomenon.

The Death of Mr. Kim

Another similar case presented the strange, fiery death of Mr. Young Sik Kim, 78. Kim, a cripple, lived with his wife in an apartment in Honolulu and unexplainably caught fire during a day in December, 1956. A neighbor found him in flames.

Mrs. Kim and the neighbors were summoned by screams and attempted to extinguish Mr. Kim, but the flames were too fierce. The Honolulu Fire Department arrived on the scene, but the fire was practically over by then.

A chair in which the victim had been sitting was destroyed, and a wheel-chair which had been used as a footstool was consumed. A venetian blind, and a clothes rack with clothes were also destroyed by the fire. In spite of the great heat that must have existed, only the corner of the room was harmed and it was merely scorched. It is immediately evident that this case is remarkably similar to the strange death of Mrs. Reeser, and equally mysterious.

More Mysterious Fires

A Mrs. M., 68, was also found the victim of a mysterious blaze in 1957. Her body, face down before a coal furnace, was so badly burned that the lower limbs were totally destroyed. The furnace was not the answer, however, for it had not been lit and was not even warm from previous fires. About the body of the unfortunate woman was a stain roughly four feet square. In close proximity were cartons, newspapers, and other combustibles, but all were untouched by the flames.

Another strange death by fire, of older vintage, was described in the *Madras Mail*, May 13th, 1907, which told of a woman who was burned to death. In spite of the obvious fact that a fire simply had to have happened, her clothes had not even been scorched. The body when found by two constables, was still smoldering. Due, of course, to the fantastic fact that the victim's clothes were unmarked by the fire, the origin and nature of the blaze remained an unsolvable mystery.

Historical Examples

A case much older was related in the *Journal de Medecin*. It occurred in Aix, Provence, France and was described by the surgeon, Muraire. During the month of February, 1779, the widow of Nicholas Gravier, a shoemaker, was found a victim of fire in her apartment.

She was described as having been of small size and extremely heavy. Mr. Rocas, a colleague of Doctor Muraire, was commissioned to make a report of the case. He stated that only a very few bones, and a mass of ashes, *calcined in such a manner that they were reduced to dust,* were found.

Only the bones of the skull, a foot, and one hand had partially escaped reduction by the flames. Very near these remains was a table untouched by the heat, and a small wooden stove was also found under the table. It was said that the grating of the stove, "having been long burnt," offered an opening for flames to have ignited the victim. This suggestion was given as a possible explanation for the mysterious fire. A chair nearby had its fore-feet and seat burnt, but other than this, the apartment betrayed no indication of the blaze that had destroyed the unfortunate woman. Rocas remarked that the fire must have burned for seven or eight hours.

Another similar example occurred at Caen. It was described by the surgeon, Merille, and was also published in the *Journal de Medecin*. Merille was requested on the 3rd of June, 1782, by the King's officers, to make a report of the fiery death of Mademoiselle Thuare. He examined the grim scene and found that the woman's body was on the floor with the top of her head resting against a hand iron eighteen inches from the fire. The rest of her body was lying obliquely before the chimney and consisted of nothing but ashes. The surgeon wrote that even the very solid bones were completely consumed and could not be identified. He stated that the two parietal bones, a part of the tibia, two lumbar vertebrae, the coronal, a part of the omoplate, were distinguishable, but that even they were so calcined that at the slightest touch they fell into dust. The right foot was intact and burnt at the upper junction. The left foot was somewhat more damaged.

Merille observed that it was cold at the time of his investigation, and there was nothing in the grate to be seen except "two or three bits" which were about one inch in diameter, and they had been charred in the middle.

He noticed that nothing in the apartment had suffered from the flames. The chair in which the victim had been sitting was found one foot from the remains, completely free of scars from the fire.

Merille noted that the woman had been a very heavy drinker, was about sixty years of age, and was very weighty. On the day of her death she had taken three bottles of wine, and a bottle of brandy.

He finally remarked that the fiery reduction of the body had taken place in less than seven hours, and again noted that nothing near the body was damaged other than the woman's clothes.

A Chinese Reference

A number of observations of considerable interest can be found in a work by M. Huc describing his experiences and travels in China.

One can hardly imagine what pleasure the Chinese

find in imbibing these burning drinks, which are absolutely like liquid fire, and, moreover, very ill-tasting. But many instances have been mentioned to us of their having died a fiery death for the sake of it; of men who have absorbed such a quantity of alcohol as to have become fairly saturated with it, and to have, in a manner, exhaled it at every pore. The slightest accident then, perhaps in merely lighting a pipe, has been sufficient to envelope those wretched creatures in flames. We have not ourselves witnessed any occurrence of the kind, but many persons, on whom we can place the most perfect reliance, have assured us that it is far from uncommon in this country.

Other Startling Cases

Another bit of odd and perhaps significant information was given before the House of Lords' Investigating Committee, July 13th, 1877, by Sir William Gull, M.D., F.R.S., Fellow of the College of Physicians and Consulting Physician to Guy's Hospital, London. Sir William's report referred to diseases resulting from overindulgence in drink.

Dr. Gull told of a case that he had personally observed involving a drayman whose body had literally become a human torch. Dr. Gull said that the drayman had been very powerful and died at about a quarter-past ten at night. The following day his body was distended with gas, and in an experimental mood, numerous punctures were made by Dr. Gull in the skin. The gas that exuded from the punctures was pronounced carbureted hydrogen, and the resultant gas jets were set afire. At one time fifteen or sixteen gas lights were burning.

In answer to inquiry, Dr. Gull said that this had happened in a number of cases. He agreed that there was a considerable amount of unconsumed alcohol in the drayman, and it was reasonable to believe that spontaneous combustion could result from excessive drinking.

Still another case quite similar was published in the Transactions of the Royal Society of London. At the time the event occurred, it was discussed in various newspapers.

Grace Pitt, the wife of a fishmonger, of the parish of St. Clement, Ipswich, aged about 60, had contracted a habit which she continued for several years, of coming down every night from her bedroom, half-dressed, to smoke a pipe. On the night of the 9th of April, 1774, she got up from her bed as usual. Her daughter, who slept with her, did not perceive that she was absent till next morning when she awoke soon after which she put on her clothes and upon going down into the kitchen found her mother stretched out on the right side, with her head near the grate, the body extended on the hearth, with the legs on the floor, which was of deal, having the appearance of a log of wood, consumed by a fire without apparent flames.

On beholding this spectacle the girl ran in great haste and poured over her mother's body some water; while the fetid odor and smoke which exhaled from the body almost suffocated some of the neighbors who had hastened to the girl's assistance. The trunk was in some measure incinerated and resembled a heap of coals covered with white ashes. The head, the arms, the legs, and the thighs had also participated in the burning. This woman, it is said, had drunk a large quantity of spiritous liquor, in consequence of hearing that one of her daughters had returned from Gibraltar. There was no fire in the grate, and the candle had burned entirely out in the socket of the candlestick, which was close to her. Besides there was found near the consumed body the

124

*clothes of a child and a paper screen which had sus-
tained no injury by the fire. The dress of this woman
consisted of a cotton gown.*

Charles Fort gives other strange examples of human
combustion and his works should be examined.

A particularly strange, fiery death of a woman named
Wilhelmina Dewar, was described in the *Blyth News,*
March 23rd-April 10th, 1908, which told how Margaret
Dewar had found her sister dead under apparently inexplicable circumstances. Her burned and charred body
was discovered on an unscorched bed, and there were no
other indications of fire, or fire-damage, throughout their
house.

It is quite possible to list case after case, which of
course is unnecessary, but I will bring our account to a
close with a very recent case which certainly seems at
the present to fall into the category of human combustion.

The *Dallas Morning News,* October 24th, 1964, described the mysterious death of Mrs. O., eight days previously. The essence of pertinent paragraphs follows:

*Police homicide detectives began an investigation to
determine the origin of a fire that suddenly turned the
former actress into a torch as she sat in a parked car.*

*Witnesses said flames had disintegrated her clothing
by the time bystanders rushed to her aid.*

*Firemen noted that the automobile itself was not
burned and that the vehicle contained no combustible
material.*

The entire subject as yet is still shrouded in mystery.
And, adding to the mystery are a number of cases involving victims who, though burned to death, were
dressed in clothing which was not affected by the
flames. I repeat this point due to its great significance

in poltergeist manifestations. Certainly no known mechanism today can explain the strange fact of unknown combustion or the poltergeist subject in general.

CHAPTER HIGHLIGHTS

On occasion humans are consumed by fantastic and mysterious fires. Many cases of earlier years are cited. No explanation yet in print or otherwise can adequately explain this mystery of combustion of humans.

chapter 13

More Mysterious Heat Phenomena

Strange Heat With Mystics

It has been said that such attacks do not harm the victims of the hauntings but a number of cases give evidence to the contrary. In fact, certain examples were cast in a malignant form showing what I believe to have been a murderous intent.

A typical example of the harmful variety was reported in the *Louth and North Lincolnshire News*, January 28th, 1905, which told the fantastic story of an orphaned servant girl who had been burned so very severely on the back that she required hospitalization. She had been "adopted" by a family and had been taken from a workshop. Certainly, the requirements for psychological tensions can be found here and the birth of a poltergeist attack was insured.

In the newspaper article it was mentioned that other abnormal manifestations had been encountered including telekinetic phenomena. The girl was sweeping a room when her employer noticed that the back of her dress was in flames. In all probability, if the blaze had not been discovered at this time, the victim would have burned to death.

It was also mentioned that a grate within the room had a small fire in it, but it was noted that the grate was protected so that it was not possible for anyone to have approached the fire too closely.

A very curious and extremely grotesque addition to the case became apparent when the farmer who employed the girl informed the newspaper that a majority of his fowls had been killed in a strange and savage way. In spite of the fact that the birds had been under careful surveillance both night and day, a few birds at a time were destroyed. The skin of the birds had been pulled from head to breast and the windpipe pulled and broken. A small number of fowls were finally left alive.

To add an odd footnote to this case, a fire had been started in a nearby chicken house a number of days previously which killed fifty-seven birds. This additional mystery also was not solved.

With these fiery attacks there has also existed another strange "heat effect" which has attracted little notice, comparatively speaking, and that is the very peculiar heat that has on occasion been witnessed in the presence of mystics. Undoubtedly, this effect cannot be restricted to the West, for we have references to mysterious warmths in Tibetan lore—the production of Tumo—which can refer to actual bodily heat as well as "spiritual" fire. Indian Mantras for the creation of fires for even such purposes as domestic use are a well-known part of the popular lore of India.

For our purpose, though, I will refer only to phenomena observed in the presence of religious mystics and saints. The strange history of the very controversial mystic and stigmatist, Palma Matarrelli, of Oria, Italy, who was born in 1825 and died in 1888, reveals an account of a presumed paranormal fire that burned during a trance, or possibly a pseudo-trance. This incident was described by Dr. Imbert-Gourbeyre who was the author of a very well-known work dealing with the subject of stigmatism. He was apparently somewhat credulous. Nevertheless, he had been a professor for many years in a well-recognized school of medicine.

Palma Matarrelli was born a peasant. She married and had three children. Her children soon died and her husband also died when she was quite young.

According to the history by Dr. Gourbeyre she became stigmatized in 1857, but in 1865 the stigmata vanished. After this event she manifested many mystical-paranormal effects, and in a sense, became a professional medium. Her psychical feats included clairvoyance, precognition, abstainance from food, and other reported marvels.

Eventually, her phenomena became suspect and her reputation tarnished. Pope Pius IX was said to have ordered an investigation of Palma's activities with the subsequent discovery that she had made use of fraud in accomplishing her miracles. Again, her history parallels the story of many notorious mediums.

In spite of these unpleasant revelations, Palma cannot be quite so simply dismissed, and her history and phenomena, real or fradulent, present a very complex and puzzling problem.

One prominent trait that Palma displayed was an eagerness to be accepted as a living saint, and she did not mind in the least publicity demonstrating her phenomena and piety. These characteristics alone gave ample reason for doubt.

The true mystic is, naturally, the complete reverse in action and attitude. The fradulent, religious mystic is as common today as in the past. I have seen quite a few specimens and in every case public demonstration of their marvels is eagerly and diligently sought. An air of piety and modesty, of course, is always assumed, but like the proverbial fire-horse and fire, when a stage is at hand the quack mystic is there.

Fr. Thurston did say in Palma's defense that she had been on occasion a good influence. It is not only possible but well-known that a person possessing genuine paranormal powers may unfortunately descend to the use of trickery at times, and it is also possible that this characteristic may have entered into the activities of Palma Matarrelli.

Dr. Gourbeyre wrote that of the four stigmatists he had personally studied, the manifestations which he had witnessed with Palma were the most remarkable. Blood which had trickled from stigmatic wounds on her forehead was caught in a handkerchief and formed strange patterns. Designs of a similar nature were burned into cloths held over her heart. The fires that created these patterns burned inside her clothes and this fantastic effect was seen twice by Dr. Gourbeyre.

As has been remarked, it is very possible that Palma Matarrelli could have fallen into the error that so many genuine mediums have slipped into, and though able to have actually created genuine, paranormal effects, still could have resorted to fraud on occasion. As stated, Dr. Gourbeyre's observations certainly seemed to have eliminated fakery at certain times, and it is indeed hard to imagine how she could have fradulently produced a number of effects that he mentioned. At the moment it seems difficult to believe that she could have created a fire within her clothes. If she had been an accomplished magician with considerable equipment available, possibly such an effect could have been managed. However, the slightest search or scrutiny would have quickly exposed the fraud. The entire problem rests upon the ability of Dr. Gourbeyre to have observed Palma's "miracles" competently.

Other Mystics

The life and death of the Dominican nun, Suor Maria Villani, provided phenomena which is considered by Fr. Thurston to have been well-verified even though a certain amount of exaggeration may have entered into the picture.

During her life she was, as has been written, constantly afire with divine love, "incendium amoris." Her entire existence was, of course, devoted to this end. It was said that due to a feeling of literal, intense heat, she drank on occasion three and one-half gallons of water during one day. According to the descriptions of those about her, when she drank the water it hissed as though it had touched hot metal.

Such a phenomena seems incredible and impossible, but after her death an attempt was made to remove her heart. An incision was made and a literal exudation of heat and actual smoke escaped from the heart, and the resulting heat was so great that several attempts were made before the organ could be extracted. A formal statement was written and signed by the two surgeons present at this fantastic happening.

Granting the reality of this reported occurrence a very interesting point is raised. The phenomena which has so often been reported with the mystics, stigmata, and the like, is generally agreed to be the result of a form of self-suggestion, so to speak. Possibly so. But what of phenomena that occurs after the death of the religious? I fear that it will be difficult to blame subconscious activity for that. And if such is done then I believe that a form of survival after bodily death is clearly admitted. A subconscious which can affect a dead body has indeed survived the grave.

During the final illness of St. Catherine of Genoa she insisted that she felt a tremendous interior temperature and as a result her hand gave her a great deal of pain. A cup of cool water was brought to the suffering saint so that she could put her hand into it for relief. Again, excellent testimony exists to this effect and also tells how an attendant who removed the cup found the water very hot.

Abnormal heat phenomena have been recorded with many mystics, and in certain cases excellent evidence exists supporting the reality of these strange manifestations, but in many ways this particular case was the most noticeable and extreme.

In spite of the fact that her death occurred during cold weather, the saint's body remained impossibly warm for thirty-three hours and only became cold after her heart was extracted and the strange incidents chronicled had taken place.

St. Philip Neri spoke many times of the fierce heat that he experienced about his heart. It is difficult to say in this case if the temperatures that he felt were subjective in nature, but it is quite possible to place him in the same category with the other heat-producing mystics.

A Dominican nun, the Venerable Agnes of Jesus, also manifested a strange heat and when she was in an ecstatic state, water was poured upon her. Again it was claimed that the water hissed and sputtered as if it had fallen upon a red-hot stove.

These very few cases that have been mentioned are not in the least isolated examples, but are given merely as representatives of their order. A number of other similar cases have existed but were not as carefully verified. This does not in the least cast doubt as to their genuineness.

Unfortunately, there are many works in existence giving the histories of Christian mystics which in spirit are very credulous and completely unscientific. As a result the physical phenomena and miraculous events described have received a rather bad name. The eagerness displayed in these works in accepting unproven, legendary, and historically unsound happenings has created resistance in many minds to even consider the phenomena which they describe.

The situation regarding works that chronicle the lives of the mystics is identical to the literature of spiritualism and psychic lore. There are the Journals and Proceedings of the American and British Socities for Psychical Research, various publications issued by organizations engaged in parapsychological studies; all devoted to scientific research and characterized by critical and demanding standards.

There are added to these publications individual books written by the many psychical researchers who have pioneered this new world. Even though a number are still considered very controversial, nevertheless they are imbued with a thorough-going scientific spirit. Many of the experiments which revealed phenomena of a major order, some of which are closely related to manifestations found with the poltergeist, are included in the list.

On the other side of the literary and scientific fence are a host of books filled with a different spirit. Some are pure propaganda works extolling dubious psychical feats and glorifying individual mediums. Some simply tell of experiences of individuals who have, according to the texts, contacted a supernormal plane. These writings, some of which are completely sincere, do not present evidence in a strict, scientific manner.

So it is with the literature of mysticism. Some works present evidence of the highest quality, perfectly eligible for scientific consideration, while other books do not display evidence which can withstand the severe scrutiny necessary for reliable documentation.

CHAPTER HIGHLIGHTS

Mysterious heat phenomena have many times accompanied mystics. Plentiful and sound evidence exists attesting to the reality of such. The same basic mechanism underlying poltergeist fires may explain the fundamental nature of heat manifestations with mystics.

chapter 14

False or Pseudo-Poltergeists

Cases of "Mistaken Identity"

Many hauntings are periodically reported which upon investigation prove to be the result of mal-observation, or lack of necessary knowledge. Fraud does not enter into such examples; that is another subject and will be discussed in a later chapter.

The traditional thermal creaks, simulated mice, banging shutters, and a host of other effects, have no doubt been responsible for many a haunted house and poltergeist, and are so well-known as to need no further treatment. Occasionally, a rather unusual case does take place which requires quite a bit of investigation to solve. One such case which happened recently has been entitled *The Phantom Phone* and proved to be a most interesting puzzle indeed.

My attention was first drawn to this oddity when I saw an article in the *Los Angeles Times*.

APRIL 23RD, 1964.

GHOST IN DEPOT
Phone Keeps Ringing but No One's There
Porterville—A ghost telephone keeps ringing in the old Southern Pacific Railway Depot there, and this is a real mystery when you consider that there are no telephones in the depot.

The rings have been heard by Al Hilton, an ardent worker for the city Museum that is to be established in the old depot building, and two workmen. The three of them said that since Monday they have heard the mysterious telephone rings as they worked to clean up the building. But a thorough search disclosed no telephones —only the empty jacks at the end of the line.

I immediately drove to Porterville and there met Mr. Hilton who proved most courteous and helpful. He described the various occasions on which he had heard the puzzling bell and mentioned that he had actually first heard it three or four months ago.

Mr. Hilton kindly allowed me to study the old depot at my leisure, but unfortunately my time was very limited, having arrived at the scene of the "haunting" at 1:30 P.M. and having to leave at 4:45 P.M. when the building was closed for the day.

While there I searched the building to the best of my ability, and, of course, found that no phones or bells existed within the depot. Just before I left Porterville to return to Los Angeles I stopped at the offices of the

Porterville Pacific Telephone and Telegraph Co. and ascertained that the last telephone and one extension were disconnected on August 12, 1962.

I should mention that while at the depot I heard several ringings at various times originating from a telephone within a gas station across the street and some distance from the building. These sounds, however, were faint and easily placed. I also heard the warning bell that rings when a car approaches the gasoline pumps, but again it was quite faint and could not have possibly been mistaken for a telephone within the old depot.

Realizing the utter impossibility of basing any conclusions upon the very scant information at hand, Mr. Ceil Smith and I drove back to Porterville on April 25th prepared to spend the entire day at the depot awaiting the ghostly and illusive telephone call. We again received permission from Mr. Hilton to study the building and entered equipped with the most vital tools of the psychical researcher, sandwiches and coffee.

Within one half-hour we clearly heard a telephone ring very distinctly and ultimately heard the odd ringing six separate times. It was fairly loud and obviously the bell of a telephone, and apparently impossible to locate. When we were at one end of the building it seemed to sound at the other end, and when we were at the other end the sound seemed reversed in position. Therefore, we were unable to find the sound's origin.

After considering the situation and the illusiveness of the ringing we decided to investigate two buildings that were to our minds the only possible source of the sound. We finally decided that a lumber yard and its several buildings must have been the source in spite of the considerable distance between it and the depot.

We entered the lumber yard and asked an employee if there were any outside telephones or bells present. He replied that there was one and showed it to us. We then asked him to ring it periodically, which he did, and we slowly returned to the depot listening for the bell. When we had reached the center of the intervening street we suddenly heard the bell ring very loudly. Obviously it could be heard within the depot.

We repeated the experiment and had the bell rung continuously as we walked from the lumber yard to the depot. After we had walked about seventy-five feet nothing could be heard. Under these circumstances the yard and office telephone which rang together could not possibly have been heard within the depot.

Therefore, we concluded that it was necessary for a wind, or breeze, to have been blowing in just the correct direction, or shift in the right direction when the telephone sounded in the lumber yard, to have produced the "phantom phone." The yard bell rang very intermittently which, of course, increased the difficulty of solving the problem, particularly when it is remembered that a wind blowing from one necessary and correct direction was essential. As I have mentioned, it was utterly impossible to fix any direction to the bell-sound within the old building and consequently what may seem to have been a very simple puzzle presented a mystery for some hours.

I must admit, I was really quite sorry when the eerie, phantom phone proved most earthly and mundane in origin. However, for every genuine case providing true paranormal effects, perhaps hundreds of pseudo-cases must fall by the wayside.

Another recent example of false poltergeist phenomena proved to be that extreme rarity—a pseudo rock-throwing. It was the subject of an article in the *Los Angeles Times*, September 21st, 1963. Mysterious rock throwings were attributed to a mischievous boy.

In this instance we have the elements of a splendid mystery. If the boy had not been apprehended the case could possibly have found its way into the literature of the poltergeist and found a niche in the category of an unproven, unsolved rock-throwing case. One interesting facet of the case was that the boy, according to the article, admitted that he was the culprit and that he had emulated other boys bent on vicious mischief. Most important of all, he gave no indications of having been familiar with the lore of the rock-throwing poltergeist.

CHAPTER HIGHLIGHTS

Pseudo-poltergeists are occasionally reported. A personal investigation by the author was made of a "phantom" telephone and a "normal" solution was found. A rock-throwing case found to be of "normal origin. Great care must be taken to prove the validity of paranormal cases.

chapter   15

Frauds Committed as Poltergeists

Fraudulent Cases Exist

Fraud has always been a problem in psychical research, and enters into the study and investigation of poltergeist-haunting phenomena as well. As with certain actions of the medium, the fradulent poltergeist-medium usually takes advantage of a moment when the observers are not on guard to toss objects about and produce other varied and mysterious phenomena. It is generally of a "telekinetic" nature, involving thrown objects, but strange sounds can be encountered. The fact that genuine phenomena is sporadic in nature, and as a rule cannot be guided or directed, obviously makes the investigator's task more difficult.

Many times fraud has started within a family home. Naturally, the families that have been victimized by the "poltergeist" are totally unsuspecting at first, and mysterious manifestations are quickly forthcoming. It has been said that children involved soon gain remarkable skill in throwing things about, and that the near-dexterity of a professional magician is often acquired.

Time is the weapon of the poltergeist-medium, for the propitious moment is merely awaited to create a mystifying effect. This feature, of course, can prove to be a complicating problem in the investigation of such cases. When a disturbed family finally becomes suspicious, or an outside observer appears on the scene, the culprit simply attempts to outwait investigation, and all phenomena ceases. When a close watch is kept unknown to the suspect, exposure will eventually occur. The suspect is trapped into producing manifestations when it is believed that there are no watchers. It may take time and a number of trials, but in the case of the fradulent poltergeist-medium exposure is inevitable. The entire process is exactly the same procedure that is used in catching the fradulent medium and requires time and patience in generous amounts.

An Entire Town "Haunted"

Perhaps the most remarkable account of fraudulent haunting and poltergeist phenomena was chronicled by Hereward Carrington in a paper entitled *A Case of the Alleged Movement of Physical Objects Without Contact.*[1] Practically an entire town in Nova Scotia entered into a conspiracy and created various types of ghostly fraud which completely fooled a spiritualist-townsman.

[1]Proceedings of the American Society for Psychical Research, Vol. I, Part II, pp. 431-519.

Objects were thrown, coins were tossed about, pipes were employed as speaking tubes, rocking chairs were set in motion by strings, and, in short, nearly everything that a busy poltergeist could do was done. Carrington visited the recipient of the hoax and soon witnessed a number of manifestations. He quickly detected the actual methods of fraud used during their manufacture. This incredible account is a must to the student of the poltergeist and psychical phenomena in general.

Accusation of Fraud Questionable

A case of considerable importance was described in the *Los Angeles Herald-Express* in 1952 and is doubly interesting for two reasons. The first is that fraud was supposedly established, and the second is that the accusation of fraud is to my mind very questionable.

LOUISVILLE, KENTUCKY, JANUARY 3RD, 1952.

Scientists from two universities joined a growing crowd today to watch objects in a local home sneer at gravity and fly around "like a shower of rain."

Two amazed county police officers swore that they saw Christmas cards, bottle caps, and a pin mysterious move from one room to another in the house last night.

Friends and neighbors flocked to the home to see the "ghost-powered" display. Police set up traffic lines to keep curious onlookers moving as reports of the phenomena spread in the neighborhood.

A physics professor at Ohio State University scoffed at the story.

A television camera set up by Station WHAS-TV to give the viewers a ghost-by-ghost account failed to record any gravity-defying movements.

Scientists from the University of Louisville, and the

University of Kentucky were to investigate the reported phenomena today.

"It's just unbelievable to all of us," the occupants said. "Sometimes just a few objects move, but at other times it's like a shower of rain with things flying over your head."

"It was unbelievable," a patrolman confirmed, and so on.

The following day a quite different story was told and according to the new article all was explained—and exposed!

All the excitement about supernatural goings-on in the tiny community died down with the unmasking of an eleven year old girl as the "ghost" of Fern Creek.

A little girl told two policemen last night she was the natural force behind the mysteriously moving objects in the home where she and three other orphans board.

She literally gave up the "ghost" by telling officers she had been lifting such objects as pencils, boxes, combs, post cards and bottlecaps and throwing them around the elderly couple's home for the past five days.

"I did it for fun and because I like attention," the girl confessed.

The case is a most interesting one and even more so for the confession that came at the end. Perhaps it falls into a special and large category featuring "exposures" and "confessions." It is a well-known fact that numerous apparent poltergeist cases have upon examination revealed fraud and exposure—and confession. In fact the pattern has become near traditional, but the picture becomes far more complex when it is remembered that perfectly genuine examples have also included confessions.

A False Confession

Such a confession was given in connection with a recent and well-attested poltergeist that infested the office of Mr. W. in California. The disturbance began on June 5 and lasted until June 17, 1964. Various objects fell to the floor, such as ash trays and telephones, light bulbs in stair wells were smashed on the stairs, a cabinet was tipped over, and typical actions of the poltergeist were well-displayed. On June 29 a person confessed that he had thrown objects around the office, but later admitted that the *exposure* was false, and a matter of *convenience*. Sufficient evidence exists to establish an excellent case and there is little reason to doubt that the phenomena observed was a genuine poltergeist.

During the Big Bear City rock-throwing case which has been described, a newspaper included a short statement from one of the occupants of the afflicted house who remarked that the stones were thrown by mischievous children, and in fact, gave the impression that the case had been solved. This was far from the truth. The police investigation resulted in an admission that the source of the stones was mysterious, no suspects were ever discovered, and a great amount of evidence of excellent quality exists describing abnormal motions and temperatures of the rocks themselves. To be exact, I consider the case a splendid one indeed and well-validated!

Except in the case of the obvious fake, exposures and confessions with the poltergeist are open to question, and at times, very suspect. To further complicate matters, a case may consist of very genuine effects, and still degenerate into open fraud. There are many reasons for this, including the desire for attention, plus a diminution of actual paranormal phenomena. I prefer to remain open to the possibility of genuine manifestations during the progress of a case, even though fraud is suspected, until sufficient fact is obtained to dismiss the incident entirely.

Natural Causes Found

Hereward Carrington studied a very interesting and instructive case in 1917 which he described in his *Invisible World* and other works. During the month of September he was asked to investigate a presumed poltergeist disturbance. When he called at the afflicted house he found the family temporarily living in an apartment in New York where they had fled in an attempt to gain relief from the unwelcome attentions of a "ghostly" visitant.

The family included three children. Carrington noticed that one child, who was ten years of age, seemed precocious and full of mischief. Various manifestations took place, but when the observers stood at a vantage point all action ceased.

Several days passed and additional phenomena were reported, but the puzzle was not solved until a friend saw the little girl seize an orange and throw it quickly across a room. The next few days provided more fraudulent activity which Carrington saw.

Ultimately, a cure was effected by the use of suggestion during the girl's sleep, thus demonstrating that such cases can on occasion be guided and cured.

Podmore, famed member of the Society for Psychical Research, was a bitter and confirmed critic of poltergeist phenomena, and physical effects in general. Apparently he could not abide the thought that such might actually exist. He contributed a well-known article to the *Proceedings* which described eleven examples of thorybistic phenomena. After examining these cases, he insisted that fraud had been proven in some and was probable in the rest.

It was Podmore's belief that the usual child involved in such cases was responsible for the manifestations, and that paranormal poltergeist effects simply did not exist. This exaggerated attitude is still quite common with many, even today, but usually is the result of a lack of knowledge and experience.

CHAPTER HIGHLIGHTS

Fraudulent hauntings are periodically exposed and children are frequently offenders. A case was investigated by Hereward Carrington during which practically an entire town produced false phenomena. A false confession was given concerning a genuine poltergeist case. However, inadequate confessions and explanations are frequently used to "conveniently" dispose of a case.

chapter 16

My Personal Experiences with the Paranormal

Personal Encounters with Hauntings

I found it a bit difficult to decide whether or not to include personal experiences in a book of this type, but finally, after considerable thought, decided that I would. Perhaps some may think that I have had, according to my account, a remarkable number of brushes with the supernormal, but it must be remembered that I have expended a great deal of effort in order to encounter paranormal activity. So, with these preliminary remarks, I will plunge in.

One of the most dramatic happenings that I have experienced took place in a house in Eagle Rock, California, June 7th, 1944. I knew the owners well, and, in fact, when I moved into Eagle Rock, heard stories about the house being haunted.

This particular event happened when I was seated in the breakfast room having coffee with Mrs. X. At 5:45 P.M. we heard some one at the front door. I heard the sound of the lock mechanism in operation and the door open. Without the least thought that anything was out of the ordinary, I automatically got up from the table to see who it was. As I started away from the table Mrs. X said, *That's only the ghost.* The oddity of the words made no impression whatsoever and I merely assumed that she was joking. I reached a small entrance hall into which the front door opened which was well lighted, and as I walked in I heard the door close. It all sounded very normal.

However, I quickly realized that the door in reality had not opened at all. It was in plain sight as I listened to the sounds of it closing, and it was obviously tightly closed. As I walked within a few feet of the door I heard three distinct footsteps walk away from the door into the carpeted hallway. In spite of the carpeting the footsteps were very audible. They were within one and one-half yards of me, and consequently were within my immediate range of vision. There was no doubt of the footsteps and there was no doubt that the walker was completely invisible. There was simply nothing to see!

I returned to the breakfast room and told Mrs. X what had happened. She then told me that this phenomenon had occurred at other times and that was why she had not bothered to answer the door. It also explained why she had said, *That's only the ghost.* Mrs. X said that the only explanation she could offer for the "ghost" was that an elderly lady who had lived next door had died, and during her life she had walked in unannounced in just such a manner. She had died comparatively recently and Mrs. X thought that perhaps the phantom footsteps belonged to her departed neighbor.

The entire incident was very impressive and I had ample opportunity to observe it under excellent conditions. The lighting was bright and I was able to hear the sounds of the footsteps clearly. There was and is absolutely no doubt in my mind that the incident was of paranormal origin.

I was told by Mrs. X's daughter, who was about seventeen years of age at the time, that her uncle had been in the habit of spending weekends at their home, and that he had complained of odd happenings in his room including objects moving about. In fact he had found the house so disturbing that he ceased his visits.

An Infested Room

I encountered a series of strange happenings in my home during the first week of August, 1953, which began with peculiar, but perfectly normal physical events, and ended with a paranormal effect.

The affair began the second day of August when I had just stacked up a pile of books on a shelf at floor level. I had just turned away when the books suddenly toppled over. Being very sure that I had merely stacked them in an unbalanced pile, I again stacked them up. After about thirty minutes or so they toppled over again. This seemed odd and I must admit that I was somewhat puzzled, but I am sure that the first pile was actually unbalanced. As to the second, I simply do not know.

In the corner of my bedroom I had a writing desk with a panel that opened from the top. When shut it completely closed the desk. The following night, a short time after I had gone to bed, the panel fell open with a loud and startling crash. I got up, closed the desk, and returned to bed. All was quiet for the rest of the night.

The next night the same thing happened again. Down came the desk-front. I slammed it shut, and no sooner had I reached my bed than down it crashed again. Considerably irritated, I shut it up, and all was quiet for the rest of the night.

As the following night drew near I wondered if my noisy desk would again repeat its startling performances, and of course it did. I jumped out of bed and jammed the desk front with a piece of paper folded to the correct thickness. Peace resulted.

In spite of my wedge, in the middle of the next night, the panel smashed down with an appalling crash. I not so cheerfully replaced the wedge, jamming it.

By this time I had become suspicious that the repeated noisy actions of the desk were possibly not quite normal. During the long time it had been in my room it had never previously betrayed any strange propensity for midnight acrobatics such as I had been treated to the previous nights. During the same hectic week I was sitting in my bedroom, reading, when I heard a loud crash at a front window. It sounded very much as though someone had thrown a stone at the glass. Fully expecting that the window had been shattered, I jumped up and examined it, and to my surprise found it intact. I went outside and looked at the ground under the window, but was unable to find any stone, or suggestion of a missile, that could have caused the sound. I was again left with a minor mystery.

The climax of this strange week finally arrived when I somewhat apprehensively went to bed and started to doze. I was brought to full awareness by most peculiar sounds that came from my hag-ridden desk. These sounds exactly duplicated the sound of a very busy hand, or hands, scratching about and disturbing the papers within. The rustling of the papers was very clear and very distinct. A hand without doubt was scrabbling within my desk. I listened intently for half a minute, or perhaps a bit longer, and the eerie noises ceased. There was, and is, absolutely no doubt in my mind that the unseen interloper was of paranormal origin.

The following morning I carefully and completely examined the desk. It was soundly constructed, and the back, bottom, and sides were solidly sealed with wooden panels. When the desk front was closed nothing in the nature of the traditional mouse could have possibly gained entrance. As a result of my examination I was forced to confirm my first impression that the sounds were not of normal origin.

The puzzling events bore all the signs of typical poltergeist activity, and the crashing sound at the window can be matched in accounts of, probably, hundreds of similar incidents.

The scratching in the desk, of course, remind us of the *hands* that scrabbled about in the somewhat questionable Cock Lane affair, the *hands* heard in the Drummer of Tedworth infestation, and many other examples. As I have remarked, the sounds that I heard gave all indications of an actual, invisible, hand in motion.

An Acrobatic Cat's Sandbox

Speaking of oddities and strange happenings suggestive of the poltergeist, I will describe a peculiar and almost ridiculous event that my wife and I witnessed Sunday morning, March 10th, 1964, which certainly had an earthy flavor. In a rented apartment we were both seated at a table having breakfast when suddenly we heard a thump as an upright, commercial, cardboard box of sand for our cat spontaneously fell on its side. It had been left standing isolated on the kitchen floor for about an hour. The box was ten inches tall, and the other dimensions were three inches by seven and one-quarter inches. It had just been purchased from a store, had never been opened, and weighed five pounds. Surprised and curious, I immediately rushed into the kitchen to examine the box. I tried every way possible to place it in an unbalanced position and found that it simply could not be done. No matter how hard I tried, the box stood firmly rooted to the floor. As one can easily see by the dimensions of the box, it had a wide, firm base, and we could not imagine how it could have possibly fallen over by itself—but it did. Incidentally, our cat was in another room at the time. So here we have a curious, and ridiculous, little incident similar to so many unexplained incidents that happen to many people, which cannot be satisfactorily explained.

A strange series of odd happenings that puzzled Charles Fort are reminiscent of the acrobatic sandbox, and these happenings are related in his *Wild Talents*. A succession of pictures fell from the walls of his home in such a manner that chance seemed excluded, and he observed that if he were not a wizard then he did not intend to allow anyone else to claim this title.

In other words, spontaneous happenings are most certainly not limited to a very few, but occur to an enormous number of people. I wish to draw particular attention to the fact that the small number of personal experiences mentioned here were completely spontaneous in nature, and probably of the same variety that Fort encountered.

I Lived in a Poltergeist House

I have had the extraordinary good fortune, from an investigator's viewpoint, to have lived in a "haunted house," and to have experienced its phenomena. Admittedly, the effects were very, very mild, and comparatively few paranormal manifestations occurred. Ghostly effects, however, are like prospecting for gold. It takes little result to pay for the thought and effort expended in the search, and the results are of great value.

The history of the disturbed house can be told briefly and simply. It was first built in 1927 and in 1928 a second addition was added. It was in effect two separate, small houses. Eventually the partition between the two houses was taken down and it became one unit.

It was rented to various people and in 1953 was occupied by Mrs. Jean Mather who experienced perhaps the first odd happenings. It is possible that earlier renters had encountered peculiar incidents, but if so, they have not been recorded.

Mrs. Smith's son, Mr. Ceil Smith, his wife and small daughter occupied it next in 1953. They stayed until 1955, and when they left, I rented it. My occupancy lasted from 1955 to 1962. The house was pulled down in July, 1962, and a large apartment building erected in its place.

After my wife and I had experienced a number of abnormal events in 1959, which I am absolutely sure were of paranormal origin, we asked Mrs. Smith if she had ever received any complaints, or heard any remarks, regarding odd and inexplicable happenings, by previous tenants.

Perhaps I should have first mentioned that her son had told me of his encounter with strange effects while living in the house, and now I was prepared to hear that others may have also observed, or heard, peculiar phenomena.

In answer to our questions Mrs. Smith replied that Mrs. Jean Mather had said she heard mysterious noises three separate times during four months occupancy, and reported one of the incidents to the West Los Angeles

Police. The police arrived in answer to her call and together with her looked completely about the house and yard. Nothing out of the way was found and Mrs. Mather apologized to the officers. She told Mrs. Smith and the police that the noises sounded as though someone were walking on the small front porch and the sound seemed to have been located near the front porch and bathroom window. Both porch and window were very close together. Mrs. Smith also told us that Mrs. Mather was a well-educated woman, employed by an aeronautical firm in a secretarial position.

The next report of unusual happenings was given by Mr. Ceil Smith who wrote a short account of an odd experience that occurred to him in 1953. Unfortunately, the exact day and month were lost, even though noted at the time; but I have a copy of his original description in my files and it follows:

About 10:00 P.M., a night after a friend, Cyrus . . . had committed suicide, I was lying in bed, but not asleep. I was brought to complete awareness by the sound of a loud thump.

Before going to bed I decided that if Cy was going to get in touch with me, tonight would be the night, and I went to bed with this thought.

Immediately following the thump I heard small noises coming from all parts of the front room, and they consisted of minor raps, creakings, and ticking sounds. These sounds had no single source, but seemed to emanate from all sides. In addition to these sounds I heard a sound that can only be described as human feet walking across the floor rug so that each foot was dragged heavily after the other one. The sounds gradually abated until all was still again.

I am certain in my mind that no normal explanation can account for these effects.

Ceil E. Smith

I well recall the impression the event made with Smith, and the detailed verbal description he gave me of the night's events. He gave me the written account on the following day. There was certainly no hesitation on his part in attributing the phenomena to paranormal causes. At the time he believed the incident was related to the death of Mr. Cyrus . . . whom we both knew as a fellow investigator.

I had lived in the house alone for quite some time before I noticed anything unusual. Naturally, the house being of wooden construction, and old for its type, possessed a good collection of creaks and snaps. After the sun had set, and the temperature had dropped, the house contracted, and loudly. I became well-versed in its schedule of creaks and squeaks. These crepitations were easily identified, and to be strictly factual, I considered the little house quite normal indeed. The thought of any ghostly influence had never crossed my mind. The strange experience that Smith had related to me, which I dutifully added to my files, was the only such incident that happened to him while living in the house. Therefore, I considered the happening as an isolated oddity, and made absolutely no connection between it and the house.

Nothing out of the ordinary happened during the first year of my occupancy, but in 1956, I began to notice phenomena that I was unable to explain normally. For example, at 7:45 P.M., March 24, I was seated in the front room reading when from the darkened bedroom came the sound of three very deliberate, heavy blows on what I believed to have been the back bedroom wall. There was absolutely no doubt that these blows were not due to any normal creakings and snappings of the cooling wood of the house; they were far too loud for that! They were, in fact, so very measured and deliberate, that one could have easily visualized an arm and fist striking the wall. As remarked, I was thoroughly familiar with the various noises of the house, and, of course, their degrees of loudness. The three blows were by far louder than anything that I had ever heard before. There simply was no comparison with normal creaks and snaps.

Another strange and exciting event happened the night of September 15, 1957, when a friend, rather than face a long drive home, decided to stay overnight at my home. He used the bedroom and I slept on a studio couch in the front room. Though the lights were out we continued our conversation calling back and forth between the two rooms late into the night. Suddenly, he yelled out in amazement and surprise, and I immediately asked him what was the matter. He replied that *something started poking in his right ear.* Beyond this nothing further happened and the rest of the night was undisturbed and quiet.

An incident that provided my wife and me with a disturbing night—a true night with a poltergeist, or haunt—was prefaced by a week of peculiar, borderline happenings that I was unable to ascribe to either normal or paranormal causes. These shadowy, half-normal, half-abnormal events are typical of psychical investigations, and can be a great trial to the researcher if they do not progress to a more advanced complex state.

Practically every night after retiring various creaks, rapping sounds, and other unidentifiable tappings, occurred. Many of the louder creaks, or rapping sounds, seemed to originate from my drawing table which I kept in a corner of the front room. The table, which I still use, consists of a heavy drawing board fastened to an iron base, and the entire construction weighs forty-three pounds. When the table is locked so that it cannot move it is creakproof.

During the nights when the borderline sounds manifested themselves, a snap or two would first be heard, and after a slight wait, still more would follow. Many of these sounds seemed to have been actual raps, but it was not really possible to differentiate between creaks and true raps. Quite frequently, these odd effects continued for as long as thirty minutes, only to cease entirely. This type of incident can be frustrating indeed, for one simply can never put one's finger squarely on the source of the sounds.

A Succession of Rappings and Sounds

During the night of December 10, 1958, I awoke at 3:05 A.M. to hear a loud creak, or rap, from the front room. Within a few minutes another occurred, and it was in turn followed by several more. They sounded exactly as though the drawing board had been lightly tapped repeatedly, and the fact that I was not in the front room at the time prevented me from attributing them to such a source. By now I was thoroughly alerted, and though still in bed, was fully conscious and attentive to the sounds emanating from the front room.

The *raps* gradually increased in frequency and intensity, and finally occurred within seconds of each other. The thought that came vividly into my mind at the time was that it seemed as though a large bird had somehow managed to enter the house, and was blundering about the room in the darkness, and in its attempts to escape was striking the walls. Obviously, the thumps and blows that were coming from the walls were being made by something contacting them physically, and by something by all laws of logic very solid.

Soon I heard clear, metallic blows, or raps, and I assumed that a long, metal, lamp that stood near the drawing board, and a stainless steel cover to a tropical fishtank across the room, were being struck repeatedly. I actually feared that the tank would be smashed, so loud were the blows. The sounds plainly originated from all sides of the room, and I realized that it was utterly impossible for any conceivable, normal cause to have created the strange disturbance. The paranormal nature of the mysterious activity was clearly beyond question.

At about 3:30 A.M., I heard an odd scuffling sound, which gave the impression that cloth was being rubbed, or scuffed, or as if dragging footsteps were crossing the rug. Still more rappings occurred, and I decided to awaken my wife so that she could share the entertainment. It might seem unbelievable that she could have managed to have slept through such activity, but I have seen her sleep through a very loud thunderstorm completely unaware the next day that anything had happened.

When I roused her, she immediately said, "Someone is trying to break in." I turned on the light and again looked at the clock. The dial of the clock was luminous and could be seen in the dark. It was 3:30 A.M. I got out of bed, the sounds ceased the moment the light went on, and went all through the house, and found absolutely nothing out of the way. After searching the house I went outside and looked carefully about the yard. Again, everything appeared normal. As a result of my investigations, I further affirmed the fact, already quite plain, that the disturbance inside the house could not be explained normally. As I wrote in my notes of the following day, *"I am quite convinced that their (the sounds') origin was definitely supernormal in nature by their frequency, loudness, and change of position."*

In 1959 my wife encountered more mysterious sounds and wrote the following note:

During the evening of January 26, 1959, I was in bed when I heard sounds of footsteps on the front porch, which I thought were made by my husband returning home. The time was about 11:00 P.M. I waited for the

familiar sound of the key turning in the lock, but heard
no working of the lock mechanism. I went into the bath-
room to look out at the porch, and before opening the
window I heard the same sound. Upon opening the
window I found no one there. I checked the house,
turned on the porch light, and looked about the house,
but again found nothing. I went into the front house
where our landlady lives and told her of the evening's
events. She then related the story of a former tenant who
had experienced the same "phenomena" several times.

Marjorie Bayless
Jan. 28, 1959

This incident is clearly a repetition of the odd sounds heard previously by a former tenant in 1953, as were the strange noises heard by me duplications of the sounds heard by Smith. A very important point is, of course, that my wife heard these mysterious sounds before either of us had heard about the experiences of the former tenant. The persistence of the phenomena is also indicated by the fact that more than one tenant had encountered the haunting.

A curious occurrence took place between 10:30 P.M. and 11:00 P.M., February 3, 1960 and involved a remarkable coincidental event related to me by Smith the following day. I was lying in bed daydreaming, as it were, when suddenly I heard a series of faint, high-pitched whistles. They seemed to be a random series of notes possessing no melody or pattern, and perhaps consisted of five to eight separate notes. At first, thinking that they must have been produced by my wife's breathing, I carefully checked and found that they continued completely independent of her breath. The strange whistles faded away and I checked the time. Nothing further happened.

The following afternoon Mr. Smith called and spontaneously described a peculiar event that occurred during the night. At my request he wrote the following note:

Last night—February 3, 1960—I heard, after going to bed, a sequence of four high-pitched whistles . . . This occurred between 10:30 and 11:00 P.M. I checked my wife's breathing, and all other possible sources for the sound, and they could not have been responsible. I am strongly convinced that the sounds were of supernormal origin.

Ceil Smith
Feb. 4, 1960

During the late evening of May 25, after retiring for the night, my wife suddenly cried out, and I immediately asked her what had happened. She then told me that she had been awakened by something jumping on her chest. She said that it felt as though it was a hand, or the feet of a cat. I turned on the light, looked about the room, and quickly went into the front room to see if our kitten, Lotus, was there. She was sound asleep on a bed that we had made for her, and was ill at the time. Due to the illness she was quite inactive, and there was not the slightest possibility that she had been the cause of whatever it was that had startled my wife. I was forced to conclude that the strange incident must be included with the other odd occurrences that we had encountered during our occupancy of the house.

Another incident of a mysterious nature took place November 23, 1960, and I again include my wife's description.

I was waiting for my husband to return home when I heard a fast drumming, or rapping, like a tapping on a window pane, or on a hollow spot in the wall, in the front room, seemingly on the window, or front door. I said, "Just a minute," and went directly to the front door and peered out the window pane in the door. Nothing was to be seen. I switched on the porch light—no one was to be seen—and at that time my husband came around a corner about fifty feet away. He had his arms loaded with groceries and this event took place at 7:15 P.M.

Marjorie Bayless
Nov. 23, 1960

A strange happening occurred late on the evening of May 14, 1961, and as did so many of these events, took place after we had retired. I was, as usual it seems, in bed thinking over the day's activities, when I heard a grunting voice apparently directly over my chest. It actually consisted of a single, short grunting sound, but nevertheless seemed to be a human voice. Nothing else transpired, and the room and the rest of the house were free of anything of a suspicious nature.

After this incident, nothing further happened beyond a number of borderline rappings, or creaks, which, though interesting, could not be considered as evidence for paranormal activity. As I have remarked, the entire haunting was very mild in nature, but in spite of its rather innocuous characteristics, it nevertheless was very real.

CHAPTER HIGHLIGHTS

Author lived in a poltergeist house and personally experienced many paranormal manifestations. Genuine phenomena occurred though mild in intensity, but still incapable of being explained on conventional scientific bases.

chapter 17

More Unusual Poltergeist Cases

Various Types of Poltergeists

In this chapter a number of unusual cases of various poltergeist types are described, some of value, and others interesting. They serve as a comparison to the examples that have been previously outlined.

The *Los Angeles Times,* March 14, 1962, included the story of a disturbed household in Indianapolis, Indiana, and the article follows:

Glassware has been breaking up all over Mrs. B's home without apparent cause—one piece even flying around a corner before shattering.

The police are baffled, and their presence doesn't inhibit the poltergeist, or whatever force is moving the glassware around. A policeman was struck on the back Monday by a glass as he was investigating.

Mrs. B . . . said it started Sunday night when a piece of crystal on top of a bookcase in an upstairs bedroom crashed to the floor about four feet from the bookcase.

Figurines, ash trays, vases, goblets, drinking glasses, and other glassware started sailing through the air and smashing.

Mrs. B, her daughter, and her mother, felt stinging pains on their arms and found small puncture wounds. They said the wounds looked like the bite of a bat.

A friend said he and his wife and Mrs. B were sitting in the kitchen when a large glass vessel sailed around a corner and shattered at their feet.

According to the description of the odd happenings, they fit well into the framework of the poltergeist. A small child was present, and barring fraud, certainly the account of the flying glassware sounds very typical. The newspaper article lacks sufficient details, naturally, to identify the case as a poltergeist outbreak, but the few instances given do imply such activity.

An Unsolved Case

Again, the *Los Angeles Times*, November 1, 1962, printed a very curious article which tells of "Pre-Halloween Mischief" at Camarillo State Hospital in California. This institution is for the treatment of the mentally disturbed.

According to the article, *The entire night shift of eleven women attendants at a unit of the State Hospital here have been relieved in favor of male attendants because of a succession of pre-Halloween pranks.* It was reported that during the last week a television in a locked room was tampered with, lights were turned on, mattresses were overturned, locked doors were opened, and "doors started shaking." It was also stated that telephones in locked offices had the receivers left off their hooks and had been used. The theory was advanced that perhaps an ex-patient had managed to obtain a duplicate set of keys and was creating the disturbance.

The very brief story aroused my curiosity and I wrote to the hospital requesting more information, and asked if anything not quite normal was noticed. I received a most courteous reply which stated this: *It is most difficult for me to associate the recently described news-*

*paper incidents at the hospital with the pursuit of psy-
chical research. Our most logical explanation of these
midnight events ascribes it to the work of an ex-patient.
There has been no continuation of this behavior.*

Considering the prevalent theory that frustrations,
tensions, and resentments foster poltergeist phenomena,
then surely an institution of this type might well be a
logical place to look for odd effects. The strange happenings at the State Hospital may have been caused
and created by an ex-patient, and yet they may not be
explained in this fashion. Whatever happened will, of
course, really remain a mystery, and a mystery which
admits of no real solution. However, we are left with an
interesting and intriguing puzzle concerning the enigma
of the poltergeist.

More Moving Objects Reported

A case rather sketchily reported occurred in Baltimore,
Maryland, and was described in the July 18, 1950 edition
of the *Los Angeles Herald-Examiner* and is of some interest.

According to the article, strange happenings plagued
a home for at least three days. The phenomena reported
consisted of objects mysteriously moved about. The occupant told the reporters that the strange effects began
when fifteen pottery pitchers "exploded" on a shelf. No
natural cause for these explosions was found.

This touched off a four-day chain reaction of weird
events. The occupant says his sugar bowl moved up
four feet from the table and deposited its contents in
the candle holders of the chandeliers, a brass incense
burner flew off a bookshelf, and ash trays fell from tables.

The article stated that no one in the family had actually seen the objects move, or fly about, but that they

had heard crashes as they struck the floor and walls and continues—

Firemen, police, and utility men have been called to investigate. All are at a loss for an explanation.

Again, we have the typical effects of the poltergeist. Assuming the correctness of the story, and the authenticity of the phenomena, somewhat minor manifestations of a telekinetic order were displayed in paranormal behavior.

Bombardment in a Print Shop

A curious and very short article was printed in the *Los Angeles Herald-Express* of July 12, 1939, which gave, unfortunately, a very brief account of an apparent poltergeist attack upon a print shop in Los Angeles. According to the story, the print shop was the target of a mysterious bombardment of little images, nails, pieces of tile, tacks, and other objects. The interior of the shop was showered by an intermittent fall, or throwing, of objects that were "constantly peppering the inhabitants from nowhere while they worked." The news item implied that the odd bombardment had lasted for several days at least.

This type of activity, as we know, is one of the more common variety, and the lack of such knowledge displayed by the article lends credibility to the incident. Indicating the lack of knowledge regarding such phenomena, the author described the word "poltergeist" as "a technical term for ghost walking." By this, I presume that he meant occasions when ghosts walk about.

A Philippine Rock-Throwing

An interesting rock-throwing case was described in *The Daily Mirror*, Manila, Philippines, October 26, 1964, and I include the article:

MARILAO, BULACAN, OCTOBER 26

Who, or what, is the unseen thing that has been throwing stones at whichever house a 14-year-old waif lived in?

Ernesto Rabanzos, who has been staying with Ilde-fonso Santos for two years since the old man's daughter picked him up in Grace Park is the object of curiosity in this little town that is all a-dither with stories of how his presence in certain houses has caused stones to rain there at night.

Among those who have "witnessed" the mysterious stone-throwing are a parish priest, former councillor, and local residents.

According to the stories, since the boy lived with the Santos family in Tabing Ilog, this town, the residence has been the object of stone-throwing seemingly by an invisible intruder.

The nuisance got to a point where it prompted Santos to file criminal action against his neighbors, whom he suspected of malicious mischief. The case was dropped for lack of anybody to accuse.

Santos finally turned the boy over to former Councillor Nemesia Santiago, a civic leader. From the day Ernesto moved in, the woman's house was also bombarded with stones.

Santiago said she could not accuse the boy of having thrown the stones himself as he was always asleep in the house whenever the strange incident occurred.

The story spread far and wide, and soon the PC and police were called in to guard the former councillor's residence. Still the things—or the stones—persisted.

Finally, the woman consulted the parish priest, who then agreed to take custody of Ernesto.

The very day the boy began staying in the convent, church windows and chandeliers were pelted with stones and at least two persons—Antonio Sumala, a scoutmaster, and Donato Fernandez, were hit.

Blessing the church to exorcise evil spirits, the priest nevertheless gave up his cause as a lost one, and said he would refer the boy to Boys Town in Marikina, Rizal.

Interested in the account, I wrote every person mentioned, plus leads that I received from Manila, but unfortunately received only one answer from the parish priest, Father A. His letter follows:

"Ernesto is now about thirteen years old. More than two years ago he had been begging in a nearby city of Caloocan. A young housewife from Marilao, Bulacan, took him into her home. He lived for two years normally with her family.

"He played with the children of his age, did errands, but had no inclination to study. He is quite naughty.

"After staying two years with the family, strange stonings happened in the house. At first, during the night, and even during the day. These things happened even with many people watching the house. The family transferred to another house of a relative, but still the stonings followed. These things continued for ten days and nights. The stones if gathered could fill half a hundred pound rice sack.

"The house is near a river—with sand and stones. The stones seemed to have come from this river, but the stones thrown to them were dry and of different sizes.

"The boy was about to be given to someone when a matron also from here took him to her family. After a

163

week . . . with this family, the stoning happened also. After some days, this family became frightened and brought him to me.

"The stoning also happened during the night, and afterward during the day. The stones fell on the roof of my rectory, and inside it so that even the window glasses were cracked. The worst stoning happened in the church. On October 20, 1964, between 8:30 and 11:00 A.M., more than one hundred stones were gathered. Many people were around.

"On November 3, 1964, I took the boy to Boys Town. Ever since, no stonings have happened at the Boys Town.

"I myself could not explain how these things happened. Who could have thrown these stones?"

A Poltergeist-Haunted Girl

A complex and interesting story was given by the *Los Angeles Times,* January 5 and 6, 1943, which described unusual phenomena witnessed in the presence of a young girl which I set out as follows:

Strange stories of unexplained happenings were told last night by a young girl, 13, who apparently has been made the object of caprice—or coincidence—by a mysterious power.

A month ago odd things began occurring in her presence. She was living with an aunt and uncle then and the family moved from their house into a hotel where the occurrences persisted.

She came to Los Angeles last Sunday, nervous and distraught, but the occurrences persisted in two homes here.

Vases and cups smash against walls and break in her

presence; ash trays are found several feet away from their proper location; a spool of thread three times flew upward from a table against a wall; a spoon apparently transferred itself from a sink to beneath a kitchen table; a bar of soap left its bathroom niche and was found on the kitchen floor.

The girl tells of these things herself and is corroborated by adult relatives, some of whom became frightened at incidents which might have been the doings of a shadow world.

It began a month ago, in the home of her uncle and aunt.

One night, she said, she and her aunt heard sounds in the kitchen. They investigated and found a date seed on the floor. They went back to bed. The noises continued, as if date seeds were dropping on the floor.

In the cupboard, a bowl full of dates was diminishing as the girl and her aunt picked up the seeds.

They first believed mice or rats were responsible. At last there were but three dates left in a bowl that had held about a dozen and one-half.

The next noise was a thud heard by them in their bedroom. This time they found the meat of a date on the kitchen floor and the seed gone.

Later that night the aunt screamed and a moment later a crash was heard. She told the girl that she had seen a pair of pliers flying through the dining room. The pliers were found on the floor.

A day later a toy glass telephone standing on the dining room table flew at the girl as she and two girl friends were walking by. Once, when she was going inside the kitchen for a glass of water, she heard a crash. Whirling around she said she saw a peach stone on the floor. There was no indication whence it came.

On New Years Eve, when the girl's bedroom became like a seance, with small objects transferring themselves from place to place and weird noises filling the air, the family moved to a hotel. Sunday, the girl went to the house of her cousin. There things began to move again.

An ash tray on a table in a room where she was sitting was found twelve feet away after everyone had heard a crash.

Two vases sitting on a table near a wall smashed against the wall and broke. A glass placed on a sofa was found broken on the floor near a wall.

The cousin, who first laughed at the girl's tales, called his nephew. When his nephew walked into the living room with two friends, a spool of thread which had been on a table thudded against the wall in back of him.

The girl, a quiet, average child in every respect, is at a loss to explain the happenings. She is afraid, though, and trembles when the incidents occur.

The following day the *Los Angeles Times*, January 6, printed another article describing a series of "tests" that were made with the girl, and according to the article, an investigator arranged a "seance" with her, and attempted to have her move various articles, such as a matchbox, a pencil, a spoon, and a card by deliberate action of her will. Needless to say, these tests failed. To have asked the girl to directly perform certain feats was nearly certain to result in failure, assuming the case to have been a genuine poltergeist outbreak.

After the experiments had failed, attempts were then made to determine if the girl had any telepathic abilities, and the tests devised for this purpose were again quite worthless. Certain tests involved placing objects in a room unseen by the girl. Later she was brought into the room and asked to locate the "target." This type of test is well-known and encourages inadvertant clues given by spectators. Results gained have no scientific value whatsoever. She was said to have done quite well.

The investigator proclaimed her an "instinctive type," and after his very cryptic remark made prints of her fingers and palms. I must admit that his action left me utterly baffled.

In spite of the lack of formal proof, of signed statements by witnesses, and in spite of the rather silly tests that were made with the girl which resulted in complete failure, the case as described is very interesting, *and has all of the characteristics of genuine poltergeist action.* Similar cases which were not scientifically investigated, or even adequately reported, still possess considerable value, and present material of definite worth for the serious thinker in resolving poltergeist action.

A Nonsensical Seance

I have been present at numerous seances and ghost hunts, that were disappointing. One example took place some years ago when I was invited to a seance with an "independent voice" medium. A microphone had been placed in the vicinity of the medium who was located in a back room. The microphone cable led into a front room where the spectators crowded around a table upon which was placed a loudspeaker. As the voices from spiritland were awaited, family quarrels broke out, various hysterical fits occurred and general pandemonium ruled. It was an unbelievable spectacle.

Needless to say, absolutely nothing took place except that the medium's stomach developed a propensity for rumbling. Each time a rumble was heard, highly amplified, the sound was loudly hailed as the spirit voice of "Uncle Swartz."

In the course of investigation, I have sat literally by the hour listening and watching professional mediums displaying "physical phenomena" not one bit more advanced beyond the nonsensical affair that I have briefly mentioned.

CHAPTER HIGHLIGHTS

Various cases and types of poltergeist disturbances are described as happening in various parts of our country. A tremendously disturbed home, a paranormal bombardment of a print shop, a rock-throwing poltergeist in the Philippines, and a haunted girl, present exceptionally dramatic demonstrations. Each case must be considered on its merits as to poltergeist activity and not human fraud as the first consideration.

chapter 18

Witchcraft and Poltergeists

Each Share Common Characteristics

The relationship between witchcraft and poltergeist phenomena presents an intriguing puzzle, and has been commented upon by various writers. There are many similarities between the two activities, and it can be suggested that witchcraft may be the child of the poltergeist. The study of poltergeist and haunting phenomena continually uncovers reminders of the close relationship existing between each subject.

A very obvious indication of the many similar characteristics of the poltergeist and witchcraft lies in the very nature of the poltergeist. As has been remarked, a picture has many times been painted which presents the phenomena of the poltergeist as the result of a playful, mischievous, invisible sprite who loves to tease its inadvertant hosts. It is thought of as a kitchen ghost producing raps, and occasionally tossing a pan or dish about, but always in the spirit of playful, though somewhat simple, fun. It has been described as the personification of the practical joker; the Till Eulenspiegel of the spirit world. Now and then this cheerful and delightful being may in its exuberance allow its humor to get a little out of hand; stones may be thrown and a window or two smashed, and other minor damage take place.

The Big Bear Poltergeist case, reviewed in a previous chapter, consisted almost entirely of rock-throwing which lasted for nearly five months, and was the subject of widespread publicity. As we have seen, numerous explanations were advanced, and most were characterized by a great lack of knowledge of paranormal actions. The *Los Angeles Times,* November 11, 1962, printed a story of the rock-throwing, which included the remark, *These are souls that have left this earth plane. They have learned on the other side how to materialize energy, and cause dishes or furniture to move.* Here we see an example of the rather prevalent belief that the poltergeist is a spirit humorist delighting in causing harmless consternation.

It is true certain accounts have hinted of happenings that perhaps seem to indicate a lighter side, but to attribute intentional humor by reason of these mere hints, so to speak, is quite questionable.

As a review of the more complex and active cases has shown, the nature of the invading force has many times been annoying and malicious, and frequently has displayed a vicious and dangerous nature. It has been suggested that in many cases the degree of malevolence can depend upon the activity and intensity of the phenomena.

For example, a mild and comparatively inactive case might offer rappings, and perhaps a few other innocuous effects.

A more active case may consist of more powerful rappings, minor movements, and stones may be thrown. Probably, the majority of poltergeist cases fall into these two categories.

At the final end of the "poltergeist spectrum," examples such as the Ringcroft case, the Drummer of Tedworth, and the haunting of a Calvados castle occur. During these infestations, the phenomena were violent and varied, and there was little doubt of the poltergeist's intentions; they were in the main savage, destructive and malignant.

It can, therefore, be seen that the poltergeist is not a teasing, playful ghost as the view stated in the *Los Angles Times* suggests.

Naturally, in former years, it was thought that such mysterious, disturbing actions of apparent, supernatural origin were due to a diabolic source, such as the workings of witchcraft. The destructive aspect so often encountered fitted well into the demonic framework, and, for example, the actions of objects paranormally moved were plainly under the control of satanic forces. The very concept of supernormal forces and actions belonged to the future, and there only remained the explanation of witchcraft. The existence of subconscious activity was unknown. Either things were acted upon by known, normal forces, or they were influenced by magical means. Magic was equated with the black art, and "white magic" was considered little better. The poltergeist—and hauntings—were shadows of the demon.

A comparison of witchcraft trials and poltergeist cases reveals many interesting similarities. Much phenomena of both activities displays alike characteristics, and, at times, the temptation to identify the two becomes quite strange. There are, though, many fundamental differences.

An Infested Child

In 1914 the story of an apparently possessed boy of eleven years of age was published in France. He lived with his father and mother in the isolated village of Molignon. He suddenly became afflicted with strange seizures which closely resembled the symptoms displayed by the victims of witchcraft and possession.

It should be stated at this point that in many ways witchcraft and possession are merely different facets of the same activity, and can, therefore, be classed together. Msgr. Saudreau remarks: *One of the most frequent causes of demonic persecution (possession) is malefice.* A malefice, or sortilege, is simply a spell cast by a witch or wizard, and therefore is a practice of *witchcraft.*

The child suffered a type of convulsion during which he jumped about, shouted, fell, rolled his eyes, and struck out with his arms and legs. To read of these peculiar seizures one can easily believe that the days of the witchcraft persecutions and terrors had returned.

During these attacks stones and sand were thrown into a room and various objects which had been placed upon a table were thrown to the floor. A friar attempted to pour holy water into a stoup, but it was broken by a rock which struck it at the moment of pouring the water. The boy was removed to a chapel dedicated to St. Anne, and here his seizures became more violent. It was remarked that two men found it difficult to hold the boy.

A blessed medal which had been strung around the boy's neck had its fastenings undone and was tossed into the air in evident disapproval by the unseen force.

Several priests attempted to aid the afflicted boy, but found that they were unable to do so. It would have been interesting to have seen what the effect of formal exorcism would have been, but judging from the account, such was not done. The phenomena and the attacks continued unabated. A well-known "white magician" was asked to dissipate the "curse." He performed various rites, including reading counter-charms from a grimoire, and he also was struck by stones while engaged in these exotic actions.

The following day the attacks and the poltergeist effects had completely ceased, and the boy was troubled no more.

Here we have a number of features common to the traditional witchcraft attack. The convulsions and frantic seizures of the boy were similar to those of persons who were presumably under magical attack. The paranormal displacement of the holy medal was quite in line with the expected traditional hatred of anything of a religious nature by demon powers. The child's parents believed him to have been cursed, and the magical cure by the magician bore out their belief.

A New England Poltergeist-Possession

The phenomena described are very reminiscent of the poltergeist-force that disturbed the home of William Morse described in the *Remarkable Providences* by Increase Mather. According to the account given by Mather, the poltergeist-medium, a young boy was frequently attacked by strange and grotesque seizures during which he was "flung about." These seizures were so violent that his parents were fearful that he might be injured. During one of the attacks the boy's grandfather attempted to hold him, but he was unable to do so because of the violence of his motions. As in the case of the French boy who was cured by outside intervention in the form of the "white magician," so was the New England child cured of his supernatural persecution by a visiting seaman.

The Amherst Poltergeist

The Great Amherst Mystery provided a combination of genuine phenomena and fraud, according to some authorities who studied the case. At the onset of the infestation, Esther Cox, the poltergeist-medium, displayed a number of physical symptoms which seemed to be of hysterical origin. However, one strange happening had a direct parallel in early cases of possession attributed to a diabolic agency.

The second night after the first signs of unnatural phenomena had been manifested, Esther and her sister had retired, when suddenly Esther cried out, *My God! What is the matter with me? I'm dying!* and bounded out of bed into the middle of the room. As her sister watched in horrified amazement, Esther's face became blood-red, her eyes protruded, and her hair stood on end. She then began to swell in size and literally became inflated. There was an explosive sound followed by three more reports, and the girl returned to her normal size. This fantastic effect was followed by other grotesque phenomena as the days passed.

A Case of Possession

A remarkable case which could well have included poltergeist phenomena, described as a case of possession, occurred in 1906-1907 in Natal. A Bantu girl, Claire-Germaine C'ele, displayed the classical symptoms of possession, including a violent aversion to anything of a religious nature. Witnesses declared that at times her stomach, or chest, became swollen, and even claimed that her neck became elongated and enlarged as though a goiter were present, and that under her skin a strange lump became noticeable and traveled over her body.

She was twice exorcised, and during the final rite, was elevated six feet from the ground, according to many witnesses. This weird effect took place in the presence of the Bishop, Msgr. Henri Delalle, Oblate of Mary Immaculate. After the final exorcism had taken place she was never again troubled.

The Loudun Possessions

The famous possessions at Loudun have been the subject of numerous writings, and do offer a fascinating study of hysteria and presumed witchcraft. As is well known, Sister Jeanne des Anges became the victim of presumed diabolic attacks, and soon afterwards the other sisters became similarly afflicted. Exorcism was used and after several hectic years the victims finally were freed from their difficulties.

The superior and a lay sister were the first to be exorcised. At the first words the superior became the subject of an attack which presented the traditional stigmata of diabolic possession. Along with the many other symptoms her face became violently distorted, and by means of her voice two fiends, Zabulon and Asmodeus, spoke. It was reported that during the proceedings her body swelled to a great size. This grotesque effect, seen in many other cases of possession, and now and then encountered during poltergeist outbreaks, resulted in the literal inflation of the body of Sister Anges. The same effect was repeated over two hundred years later in the seizures of Esther Cox.

In 1746 the possessions at Loudun were paralleled at the convent of Unterzell. A nun became the victim of hysterical symptoms including hallucinations of touch, sight, and hearing. Crampings occurred and significantly her body became greatly swollen.

This case, however, offers some evidence for the presence of poltergeist phenomena. Stories were told that the convent was haunted by strange and varied effects. It was said that animal sounds were heard, ghostly laughter occurred, and phantom figures were seen at night. More to the point, it was also claimed that furniture was moved by unseen forces, and chairs turned over mysteriously. A large oak chest was upset with a crash that alarmed the convent.

Eventually, other nuns fell prey to possession, and screamed, foamed at the mouth, and manifested the usual hysterical actions of presumed demonic attack.

Judging from the accounts of the disturbed convent, and the actions of the originally afflicted nun, there may have been actual paranormal phenomena mixed with the hysterical flights of fancy which resulted in the neurotic seizures of the nuns who believed themselves possessed.

The case is similar to the Amherst case in that the nun who first manifested the actions of possession was also mysteriously and grotesquely inflated, and probably the focal point of the disturbance. Unfortunately, in cases of this type, exaggeration played its part, and beliefs of the time crept into contemporary accounts at the expense of fact.

Strange Bitings on Persons

Another interesting effect common to both witchcraft and the poltergeist is biting. Andrew Land mentioned in *Cock Lane and Common Sense* the case of a woman who was bitten upon the shoulder and upon the thumb. She was seized by invisible teeth when she threw holy water under a chair.

An extremely interesting example of biting poltergeist is included in Fr. Thurston's *Ghost and Poltergeists*, entitled, "An Account of Disturbances, etc., at the Lamb, Without Lawford Gate." Many violent effects took place, including objects thrown about and a variety of scratchings and knockings. Two children were apparently the focal point of the infestation, and they were repeatedly bitten, pricked with pins, and received mysterious cuts. During one particularly active and unpleasant day one of the children's arms was examined and forty cuts, old and new, were seen and counted. A close tie with traditional witchcraft became noticeable when the children claimed that an apparition, the figure of an old and raggedly dressed woman, was responsible for the strange persecutions. The date of the poltergeist disturbance was the year 1762, and, as Fr. Thurston observed, the apparitional old woman merely reflected the beliefs of the period. Pins, of course, were favorite instruments used in witchcraft spells.

During the poltergeist attack upon a woman, an account of which was included in Increase Mather's *Remarkable Providences*, bitings were frequently encountered. According to the account, on one occasion as she entered her house, she *was bitten on both arms black and blue . . . the impressions of the teeth being like man's teeth were plainly seen by many.* In spite of certain obvious exaggerations, the case strongly suggests that real paranormal phenomena did occur.

The Witchcraft Terror of Salem

During the witchcraft terror at Salem, New England, on March 24, 1692, a number of witnesses appeared before the magistrates who were examining a suspect accused of witchcraft. One self-styled victim of diabolic attack claimed that the suspect caused her to have been bitten, and in proof exhibited the marks of teeth upon her wrist.

At the trial of Bridget Bishop, several of the "bewitched" testified that she, or rather the *shape of the Prisoner did oftentimes very grievously Pinch them, Choak them, Bite them. . . .*

One curious observation given in the account of her trial stated that as she passed the meeting house of Salem while under guard, she looked at the building with the result that, *A Demon invisibly entering the Meetinghouse, tore down a part of it; so that tho' there was no person to be seen, yet the People, at the noise, running in, found a Board which was strongly fastened with several Nails, transported unto another quarter of the House.*

The trial of Susanna Martin included testimony by Jervis Ring who claimed that he was persecuted in the night, but was unable to see who was troubling him. Finally he saw the accused come to him, and as she did she bit him upon the finger. According to Ring's statement the incident happened seven years previously. Obviously, standards of evidence were near-devoid of common sense!

Rev. George Burroughs was brought before a special

court and was found guilty of witchcraft. Various witnesses made the usual accusations, including the claim of supernatural biting. Mather states:

The Testimonies of the other Sufferers concurred with these; and it was remarkable, that whereas Biting was one of the ways which the witches used for the vexing of the Sufferers; when they cried out of G. B. Biting them, the print of the Teeth would be seen on the Flesh of the Complainers, and just such a Set of Teeth as G. B.'s would then appear upon them, which could be distinguished from those of some other Men's.

Here we have a definite statement that biting was a recognized method of attack in old New England. It is an interesting observation, and shows that it was more in the nature of a widely known effect, rather than merely the accusation of a few particular witnesses.

Rev. Burroughs was undoubtedly a remarkable man. He had written a paper which insisted *That there neither are nor ever were Witches, that having made a Compact with the Devil, can send a Devil to Torment other people at a distance.* Naturally, these opinions must have sat ill with the community and undoubtedly contributed to his destruction.

The fact that actual poltergeist phenomena had been observed about the same period must have provided fuel for the fires of the witchcraft trials. A more unfortunate coincidence could not have occurred.

False Apparitions

Very possibly, the frustrations and fears brought about by fanaticism and a restricted, narrow, fear-filled way of life created tensions aiding the liberation of the poltergeist-force.

During the witchcraft trials in New England a good number of the descriptions given by the self-styled victims of magical attack furnished claims that they were struck, choked, troubled by fearful apparitions, taken by strange seizures, and a host of other grotesque effects. Obviously, there must have been a goodly number of hysterics who actually underwent self-imposed torments. However, the majority of the "victims" were plainly motivated by fears, revenge, and envy, and many seized upon the opportunity to destroy those whom they disliked. A number of the accusers must also have fallen in with the majority, for they knew well that if they had attempted to aid an accused individual, they in turn would have been in grave danger of suffering the same fate.

Many of the attacks described by those who had played the part of witchcraft victims provided invented phenomena for the purpose of reinforcing their accusations. The descriptions of the apparitions that were supposedly seen were childish, and their actions were infantile, and had little value as evidence for paranormal activity. They can easily be dismissed from any serious consideration.

A typical description of such an "apparition" was given by John Louder who testified against Bridget Bishop in the witchcraft trials. He claimed that *Immediately after, sitting down, he saw a black Thing jump in at the window, and come and stand before him. The Body was like that of a monkey, the Feet like a Cock's, but the Face much like a Man's.* This childish conception spoke saying that Louder would want for nothing in this world if he would accept the phantom's rule. The offer made by the demonic figure was very typical of the remarks attributed to these beings, and such were frequently quoted at the witchcraft trials. The deliberate intent of the witnesses to invent demons was borne out by the ridiculous descriptions given. It does seem incredible that such nonsense was considered as serious evidence, but we have equally ridiculous nonsense exhibited today in many spiritualistic gatherings.

For example, I have actually sat in a dark seance and have been told in all apparent seriousness that the room was literally filled with visible spirits. In fact, I was informed that one very sociable spook was sitting on my lap. Needless to say, there was absolutely nothing to see, but my spiritualist visitors, three, I believe, were all able to easily see and converse with our phantom band. This ridiculous seance can be matched and surpassed today in any "physical" seance.

The fits, seizures, and trances manifested by the victims of witchcraft attacks were similar to the behavior of a number of poltergeist-mediums. A certain amount of this similar action was due to the poltergeist-medium's familiarity with traditional witchcraft lore.

Frequently, the witchcraft victims were convulsed, ran about with superhuman energy, became rigid and cataleptic, threw themselves about, and demonstrated abnormal strength. Obscene language, blasphemy, and altered speech were part and parcel of such possessions. Trances and seizures identical to those seen with a number of genuine poltergeist-mediums have been observed however, which I believe were not due to the medium's knowledge of witchcraft lore.

With the phenomenon of possession we are dealing with a significant subject providing material of value. In spite of the obvious fact that the majority of the symptoms of possession were of hysteric origin, still certain cases have displayed paranormal phenomena. Well-authenticated cases of "possession" are difficult to distinguish from a certain class of poltergeist outbreak, as we have noted, and in great part must originate from the same source. The theology of the "demons" speaking through the mouths of the possessed is most orthodox, and clearly is molded by the beliefs of the afflicted.

An example of possession and witchcraft which is of great interest began in the year 1864 and ended in 1869, and occurred in the village of Illfurth, France. The victims were two young brothers, Thiébaud and Joseph Burner, aged nine and seven respectively. The typical and traditional symptoms of possession were manifested and doctors were baffled. The brothers whirled about on their backs at fantastic speed, suffered odd convulsive seizures during which their arms and legs were subject to distorted positions and motions, and on occasion became rigid for hours. Frequently, deafness occurred, and they often shouted and yelled obscenities. It was also said that they were able to speak and understand several languages. Each brother was possessed, presumably, by two devils, and, of course, the incredible and fantastic actions and speech were attributed to these evil beings.

It was soon discovered that the children's seizures became greatly intensified when in the presence of rosaries, holy medals, and the like, and they demonstrated hatred when any mention of the Virgin Mary was made.

Various paranormal manifestations were claimed. These claims included the ability to predict forthcoming events, discuss subjects out of keeping with their ages and education, and it was also said that at times when they were seated, chair and sitter both were levitated.

The children were finally exorcised and relieved of their fantastic malady. During the course of the exorcism the children's symptoms became more exaggerated, and one boy had to be confined in a strait jacket on one occasion, so violent were his contortions.

The case of Hélène Poirier presents many similar effects, and it seems quite probable that in her case actual poltergeist phenomena were encountered. During a night in the year 1850 she was awakened by a number of startling rips. As they continued they increased in intensity until they became powerful blows. A search was made in her room and nothing unusual was found.

A few months after this strange incident Hélène fell rigid to the floor repeatedly. As time went on her symptoms became more pronounced, and finally it was believed that she was a victim of demonic possession. In the month of August, 1867, a number of witnesses insisted that she had been levitated two different times, and according to the account given in Msgr. Cristiani's work, had been raised into the air numerous times.

She often had the same experience as St. Vianney when the curtains of her bed were shaken, and the curtain rings run back and forth for hours at a time. Twenty witnesses testified to this effect. She suffered slaps, kicks, and was said to have been pulled about by the hair.

It is quite common to read that victims of possession were struck, pulled about, and thrown to the ground, but as was not known in previous years, a subject during hysterical seizures may duplicate such apparent actions without normal awareness. Probably, Hélène's physical phenomena, excepting the reported raps, were of this nature. The rappings, and levitations, may have been another matter.

Her seizures were frequently extremely violent, and were, apparently, identical to those of the Burner brothers. On one occasion, for example, during exorcism, she foamed at the mouth, was subject to the most distorted contortions, cursed, asked assistance from hell, and finally broke away from those attempting to restrain her and threw furniture about. Finally, two last yells were given and she passed into a sleep from which she awakened free from her torment.

It was also stated that during her seizures she was capable of conversing in Greek and Latin and was able to answer difficult and learned questions in theology. It would be interesting to know whether or not she had been exposed to these languages, and so had acquired the use of them subconsciously. However, the mere repetition of presumably unknown words is one thing, but ability to weave them into useful sentences is another, and hardly explainable by subconscious acquisition. This point, unfortunately, has not been made clear, and it is useless to speculate.

She was subject to further demonic attacks at intervals until her death in 1914.

It can be seen that Hélène Poirier's seizures were near-identical to those of the two possessed boys including the claim that unknown languages were spoken. If it were not for the fact that, at times, evidence for the existence of poltergeist phenomena was present, the victims of possession could easily be dismissed as hysterics. The phenomena described fit well into this category, but when paranormal effects are reported the picture changes. However, it can be seen that possession and poltergeist mediumship are closely related.

The phenomena of possession is not a thing of the past, and, for example, is still considered today by an orthodox church to exist. A very interesting case has been reported covering a period from 1950 to 1959, and perhaps may still be in progress. Many other churches accept the concept of possession and utilize various forms of exorcism.

Many churches espousing a fundamentalist creed insist that possession is a fact, and the Spiritualist movement has long insisted that this phenomenon is very real. I might add that I have seen an ad repeatedly in a spiritualist publication which claimed that evil spirits were dispossessed; in fact, this was the "star turn" of a particularly gifted medium. On one occasion I watched a medium "exorcise" several unwanted spirits, and the evening was climaxed by the participation of "Christ." Such truly distasteful and irreligious performances are fairly common with a few professional mediums.

A Recent Case of Poltergeist-Possession

A remarkable case of possession was reported in the province of Ninh-binh, Tonkin, (North Vietnam) at Phat-Diem, in 1924-1925. The author of the report was Msgr. de Cooman. The report tells of the persecutions of a young novice which began with showers of sticks and stones, and violent blows. Other phenomena included all types of thrown missiles; bottles, bits of wood, potatoes, and numerous strange sound effects: laughter, sobs, bird cries, among others.

Finally, the other novices suffered a contagious possession, attempted to climb trees, and manifested other various strange actions. Ultimately, fourteen persons became possessed, and exorcism was undertaken. Peace finally descended upon the distubed convent.

It does seem that the outbreak included genuine poltergeist phenomena. Without doubt, the beliefs of those involved caused the phenomena to be interpreted as due to demonic intervention, and resultingly, hysterical contagion occurred. Here, then, we have a combination of probably supernormal effects, and belief in witchcraft, with the result that the case was described as an example of devilish possession.

Comparison of Poltergeists and Witchcraft

The grandiloquent speech that has been reported rarely with the poltergeist is very similar to that of the presumed demons mentioned in witchcraft trials, and also has a great resemblance to many communications received via the planchette writings.

The phenomena of the poltergeist and the pseudo-phenomena of witchcraft and possession have many similar attributes, but also have many differences. The chief difference, naturally, is the general lack of paranormal effects to be found with witchcraft. We are not now considering the coincidental—and probably genuine—poltergeist cases that took place, for instance, during the New England witchcraft terror. The reported magical phenomena bore little resemblance to genuine paranormal effects, and this fact alone is sufficient to dismiss most witchcraft tales as of slight worth. Their value lies in being psychological studies and oddities, and little else.

Another essential, though obvious, difference is that witchcraft was, and is, a system involving deliberate techniques for the production of desired effects. The "system" is a loose, poorly defined one, and one that varies from country to country and year to year. Nevertheless, definite routines have existed and do exist to bring about certain effects, and by adhering to the proper formulas particular results are theoretically forthcoming.

Poltergeist and haunting phenomena, on the other hand, are almost completely spontaneous in nature, and cannot be produced at will.

In general, it can be said that the phenomena of the poltergeist have a very superficial resemblance to that of witchcraft, and occasionally, as in New England, actual paranormal manifestations coincidentally occurred.

An interesting case illustrating the point took place in 1661 in Ireland. A "witch" named Florence Newton greeted a girl, Mary Longdon, with an apparently affectionate embrace and suggested that they be friendly with each other. Shortly afterward the girl insisted that she saw a strange woman wearing a veil, and when the veil was removed she saw that it was Florence Newton. Grotesque seizures followed consisting of trance-like states, "fits," etc., and mysterious physical effects occurred. Stones were thrown, furniture was moved about, and feather beds fell upon her. Florence was brought to trial but no record exists telling what decision resulted.

Many features of hauntings were undoubtedly incorporated into witchcraft lore. One extremely interesting belief found with witchcraft was the conviction that the witch was able to project her "shape" at will to any destination desired. I suggest that this belief may be related to the phenomena of bi-location, or ESP projection, and is worthy of further study.

During the poltergeist cases that occurred simultaneously with witchcraft outbreaks—I assume that a certain number of these cases were genuine—the poltergeist mediums undoubtedly copied many of the traditional actions of the victims of diabolic attack, which, of course, increased the apparent similarity of the two activities. Due to the prevailing beliefs, such mimicry was really unavoidable.

The subconscious, as has been indicated, determines in great part the poltergeist and haunting phenomena. As a result much of the grotesque element that appears often is explainable. The dreamlike characteristics that have been encountered bear this thought out. In fact, it has been said that, at times, many cases can be likened to a material projection of a dream.

The malice shown by the poltergeist is again explainable in large degree by subconscious activities. The frustrations and repressions that shape much of our dream material similarly mold paranormal phenomena.

Many of the practices of witchcraft were of a nature that aided the creation of trance states, and herin lies the possibility that the occasional witch endowed with paranormal abilities could well have released psychical forces. Inasmuch as evil intent played a large part in such a person's life, any paranormal effects produced surely would have been colored by her emotions and beliefs. Resultingly, phenomena of an unpleasant and undesirable type could have occurred.

CHAPTER HIGHLIGHTS

A close relationship exists between witchcraft and the poltergeist. An account of a haunted-possessed-child, the Amherst haunting, cases of possession, and bitings characteristic of the poltergeist and witchcraft, and New England witchcraft trials have been analyzed to show the relationship of witchcraft and poltergeist.

chapter 19

Exorcism and Poltergeists

Can The Poltergeist Be Exorcised?

Various forms of exorcisms have been used throughout the centuries to combat what were believed to have been incursions of undesirable, supernatural forces. Very probably the best known form of exorcism is that which has been used to deal specifically with demonic possessions. The Roman Catholic church, however, utilizes another such rite although it is not usually thought of as such. This exorcism takes place during the ceremony of baptism and includes the words, *I adjure you, unclean spirit, in the name of God the Father, omnipotent, and in the name of Jesus Christ, his Son, our Lord and Judge, and through the power of the Holy Spirit, that you relinquish this creature of God, which our Lord has deigned to choose as His holy temple, that it may become the temple of the living God and that the Holy Spirit may dwell in it.*

It has been thought by many that the Roman Catholic church employs a form of exorcism for the cleaning of infested or haunted houses. However, as Fr. Herbert Thurston mentioned in his *"Ghosts and Poltergeists,"* no provision exists in the ordinary service-books for cleansing such dwellings, but he did find a ritual published in Madrid in 1631 which is entitled *The exorcism of a house troubled with an evil spirit.* This rite is little known today.

Many other churches have sanctioned the use of prayers and rituals for this purpose, and these as such are definite rites of exorcism. The use of prayers and ceremonies to deal with ghostly powers are, of course, world-wide and ageless.

The efficacy of exorcism and religious rites upon the poltergeist has often been questioned. In *Can We Explain the Poltergeist?*, Dr. A. R. G. Owen writes that rituals of exorcism have given beneficial results and have ended cases. He also notes that on occasion religious rituals and objects seemed to have increased the poltergeist's fury and destructiveness.

Harry Price, a noted British authority, stated that, *My opinion is that poltergeists cannot be exorcised—with exceptions!*

The Mechanism of Exorcism

In spite of the fundamental mystery that shrouds the enigma of the poltergeist, certain tentative suggestions and explanations can be advanced which do shed some degree of light upon the mechanisms behind the ghostly forces' response to exorcism. One obvious clue is the great part played by subconscious activity. Generally malicious and frequently destructive outbursts of phenomena have been traced to unhappiness, resentment, frustration, and tensions in general existing within the inadvertent poltergeist-medium. Resultant effects are, therefore, a paranormal extension of normal abilities, acting as a release for tensions, and may even possess certain psychologically curative properties.

With this background in mind it can be seen that inasmuch as the birthplace of the poltergeist is found within the unconscious then the key to controlling this force through exorcism is suggestion. The necessary forms of suggestion capable of modifying and even ending these psychological eruptions are easily found. They lie within social traditions, and perhaps most important of all, within the compass of religion.

I believe a general rule may be stated: *Proportionate to the degree that custom and religious beliefs are established within the unconscious, so will the phenomena of the poltergeist be subject to exorcism.* This is conditioned by the degree of psychological tension, and resultingly the intensity of phenomena will vary from modified and diminished activity to complete cessation.

Another factor is still more complex and hinges upon the question of survival of death and spiritistic intervention. If in certain cases discarnate influence exists, then the intensity of phenomena may depend upon the degree of religious beliefs of an intervening spirit, and the factors mentioned in the preceding paragraph directly apply.

Further, religious factors similar or identical to those encountered with the activities and phenomena of mysticism may also apply, but these last are even more mysterious and speculative from a scientific point of view. Nevertheless, such possibilities should be kept in mind.

Cases may also exist that include part or all of these factors. The entire problem of poltergeist phenomena and exorcism is a demanding one and admits of no simple and quick solution.

Comparison of Cases on Exorcism Rites

A very early observation was given by Giraldus Cambrensis in about the year 1191 which mentioned that poltergeist-hauntings were unaffected by holy water, and similar religious implements.

It is my opinion that religious rituals do have a definite influence upon some of these disturbances, but that other cases are either unaffected, or the poltergeist is roused to more activity.

A very remarkable case entitled "An Indian Poltergeist" in Fr. Thurston's collection of writings was marked by a ferocious hatred for all matters religious by the infesting force. Sacred pictures were torn, religious medals were taken away, crucifixes were thrown about, and on one occasion a crucifix was placed in a fire and damaged, and other actions of a like nature performed.

It must be noted, however, that during prayers the disturbance ceased, but resumed immediately afterward. This action is very characteristic of the poltergeist and has been noted in numerous cases.

A novena was finally carried through in honor of St. Joseph, invoking his aid, and the novena was finished on a March 19. On this day, writings were found on the walls of the bathroom which said that the "devil" had left, and all disturbances ceased. As had been mentioned earlier, the poltergeist seemed to have a curious preference for writing in the bathroom. It does seem that in spite of the infesting poltergeist's indifference to a previous display of religious objects, this last ceremony was efficacious.

During the famous haunting of a Calvados castle, given in Flammarion's *Haunted Houses,* the ghostly invader manifested a dislike for religious matters.

We went into the Abbé's room, which had been locked, and found all his books, at least a hundred, strewn over the floor. In the midst of this vandalism only three books were left standing in the shelves. *These were books of the Holy Scriptures.*

During another day, a number of religious medals and a cross which had been attached to a door were missing. A few other objects in the Abbé's room had also been slightly disturbed.

On still another day a visiting priest made a special ceremony and for two more days the castle was almost quiet. A few mild noises were heard, but on the third day new phenomena occurred which was fully as violent as that which had preceded it.

Eventually, a Novena of Masses were said at Lourdes and according to the text, *The Reverend Father has made the exorcism and everything has stopped.*

A few months later, however, the phenomena renewed its activity. Nevertheless I do think that in this case the religious rite mentioned obviously had an effect even though not lasting.

During another very interesting infestation the aid of a curate was asked, and when he heard the nature of the haunting he remarked that it was of little importance and was probably due to the age of the house, and the fact that it had not been blessed for a long time. He then said that if further trouble was encountered, he would bless it. *From that day the noise ceased entirely.* Again, it is very clear that a religious rite, so to speak, ended the disturbance.

Another case given by Professor Flammarion included bell ringing of a mysterious nature. A priest, who was sent for, blessed the disturbed house, but in spite of the rite, the phenomena continued.

After some time a young servant girl sixteen or seventeen years of age left the house with her father who was reputed to have been a sorcerer. Before they left the father made an incantation *to drive the evil spirits from the house,* and all was quiet afterwards. It is very possible that the girl was actually a poltergeist-medium and the phenomena ceased with her departure, but it is also possible that the "exorcism" was responsible.

Exorcism played a very definite part in the possession of Hélène Poirier. Poltergeist phenomena seemed to have been present in this case as we have read. She was exorcised at least twice in six years and these exorcisms had definite effect.

During the possession at Phat-Diem which has been described and which proved contagious, the manifestations centered about a young novice, Marie Dien, and according to accounts, genuine paranormal phenomena occurred. The novice was exorcised, as were other novices, and complete peace resulted.

The A. rock-throwing case in New Zealand, described in an earlier chapter, presented a rather exotic exorcism that apparently was very successful. Mr. A. related the strange story to a reporter and the following account was published in a New Zealand newspaper, *The Evening Post.*

. . . *a Samoan knocked on our door and insisted on*

speaking to me alone—there were no police in the house at the time.

The Samoan told me that I had made a terrible mistake when I cut the trees down in front of my house. He explained that I had left the trunks far too high and they could be seen from far off . . .

These things represented something evil, my Samoan visitor added, and he implored me to have the tree trunks cut down to ground level. After giving the matter every consideration and prepared at this stage to try anything, I finally arranged for the trunks to be cut.

Then a very strange and significant thing happened to us yesterday. An elderly Maori woman and a youth arrived at our house and told us that they came from a long way to rid the house of the evil spirit who was throwing the stones.

The woman gave us exactly the same explanation as the Samoan. The trees had to be cut to ground level for an evil spirit hid in the trunk. Assisted by the young Maori, the woman then proceeded to rid the house of all evil spirits. She had bread and potatoes with which she said she would feed the evil spirits and thus get rid of them. Then, with blessed water, the old lady went into every room in the house three times and spread the water.

She then went outside and knelt on the grass to pray. When she had finished the praying she announced to me that there would be no more trouble from evil spirits and there would be no more stone throwing.

The stone throwing ceased!

I also received a letter from Mrs. A. which corroborates the newspaper article.

In this interesting case we have an exorcism and added instructions regarding the "offending" trees, and when both had been accomplished the phenomena came to an end.

Trees also played a curious part during the very probable poltergeist case which was reported in New England many years ago. Increase Mather writes about it in *Remarkable Providences* as follows:

I am further informed, that some (who should have been wiser) advised the poor woman to stick the house round with bayes, as an effectual preservative against the power of evil spirits. This counsel was followed; and as long as the bayes continued green, she had quiet; but when they began to wither, they were all by an unseen hand carried away, and the woman again tormented.

There does seem to be some relationship between the phenomena of this last example and the previous case. In the New England infestation, however, other complex manifestations apparently were encountered. The planting of the trees constituted an "exorcism," in a sense, and the action was effective according to the account.

I will now list a few cases which provide phenomena unaffected by exorcisms, beginning with the well-known example that occurred in Turin, Italy, and was investigated by Prof. Cesare Lombroso. Various types of phenomena were observed, including paranormal movements of objects and the famed misbehaving wine bottles encountered by Lombroso. He wrote that neither priest nor the police were of aid.

Again referring to the Rabanzos case in the Philippines, *The Daily Mirror of Manila* stated:

Blessing the church to exorcise evil spirits, the priest nevertheless gave up his cause as a lost one, and said he would refer the boy to Boys Town in Marikina, Rizal.

During the Ringcroft disturbance (1695) there is no doubt that the exorcism was not effective. In a tract written by Alexander Telfair and printed in the year 1696, the trials and failure of five ministers to cleanse the invaded house were described.

Prayers proved equally ineffective during the "Drummer of Tedworth" disturbance. During "Prayer-time" the poltergeist would diminish its activities, but resumed its attentions immediately afterward. For example, after prayers a minister who had attempted to aid the afflicted family was hit on the leg by a bedstaff, but the blow proved to have little force behind it.

Ballechin House of ghostly fame was at one time "exorcised," but again to no avail. The rooms were sprinkled with holy water and a special prayer said. At a later date a Catholic Archbishop attempted to allay the ghost, but he also met with failure.

Eleanore Zugun, who was the subject of great scientific interest in the 1920's, was early in her career as a poltergeist-medium, exorcised, and was the center of various religious actions, but the infesting force remained, nevertheless.

During the course of the Poona poltergeist case, detailed by Fr. Thurston, prayers apparently increased the activity, and the poltergeist, interestingly, displayed an equal dislike when a mantra was said. As in "An Indian Poltergeist" case, the invading force was annoyed by the Hindu "exorcism."

During the course of the well-known Derrygonelly haunting investigated by Sir William Barrett a Bible was moved about, and attempts by a Methodist teacher (the family were Methodists) to banish the poltergeist proved futile.

It is possible to add case after case to this brief list, but these few examples illustrate the relative effectiveness of various rituals. As is easily noticed when reviewing large numbers of such disturbances, a goodly percentage fall between the two extreme results of exorcism; failure and success. These examples are marked by a response of the poltergeist to prayer and rite in that quiet or diminished activity results for a time but is resumed later. In a sense such response indicates a certain degree of amenability to religious action.

Multiple Personality and Poltergeists

The relationship of secondary and multiple personality to poltergeist phenomena is very noticeable, and a perfect example is provided by the Doris case of multiple personality. During the early part of the treatment of the case Dr. Walter Franklin Prince tried exorcism three times, believing that perhaps this might be an effective kind of treatment through suggestion. He also wished to include the possibility of a spiritistic obsession. The "Margaret" personality, alike in many ways to the poltergeist although not possessing paranormal abilities, reacted with violence and remarked, *"You'll lose D., you'll lose D., if you don't look out.*[1]

The Doris case is so generally considered to be an example of multiple personality and nothing more that it might be well to mention that Dr. James Hyslop conducted a series of experiments with Doris and the medium Mrs. Chenoweth to see if paranormally received information might be gained. Evidence was obtained, and Dr. Hyslop considered that the results fitted well into a spiritistic category.

As we can see, exorcism on occasion does definitely work, and yet on other occasions it frequently fails. As remarked previously, a large percentage of cases fall

[1]W. P. Prince, "The Doris Case of Multiple Personality," Proc. A.S.P.R., Vol. 9, 1951, p. 312.

into the middle ground in that exorcism may in the long run prove futile, but it still has a certain effect upon the poltergeist-force.

Final Theories

As to final explanations—that is for the future, I believe. It does not seem that sufficient knowledge has been obtained to make any "final" pronouncements. We do know that subconscious phenomena play a very large part in poltergeist effects. As in secondary personalities and multiple personalities a "self" is manifested that frequently is malicious—and malignant on occasion. Therefore, many parapsychologists consider the poltergeist to be a form of secondary personality plus abnormal, psychical powers. This theory, of course, finds no need to consider any possibility of spiritistic origin or influence. But, as the Doris case indicates, the possibility of spiritistic influence is by no means eliminated. Again, the element of bi-location, or out-of-the-body-experiences, bears directly upon the entire problem, for if such experiences imply, or prove, survival (and I believe that they do) then a spiritistic element may enter into certain cases of poltergeists.

CHAPTER HIGHLIGHTS

Various cases of exorcism have been compared and examined. A Maori exorcism performed during a New Zealand rock-throwing proved efficacious. Exorcism to dismiss poltergeist does at times have desired effect. Multiple personality and poltergeist is very noticable, and may be fitted in to a spiritistic category. Many parapsychologists consider poltergeists to be a form of secondary personality having abnormal and psychic powers.

chapter 20

Saints and Poltergeists

Mystics Prone to Hauntings

The lives of the Catholic saints and mystics are rich with hints and accounts of supernormal phenomena and poltergeist lore. The saintly mystics were prone to ghostly infestations which were entitled diabolic attacks, and an extensive study of their lives would uncover an amazing number of hauntings and poltergeist outbreaks. In many cases testimony came direct from the mystics themselves, and as witnesses of integrity, their honesty and sincerity would hardly be questioned by even the most vigorous skeptic.

The very nature of the saint implies a mediumistic bent. In the case of the more emotional mystics, hysteria and dissociated phenomena were present during much of their lives, which favored the emergence of paranormal effects. The tendency to extreme suggestibility could only have been conducive to such phenomena. Dissociative characteristics are not considered detrimental in nature, but are thought to be necessary attributes for the development of the mediumistic personality.

Under the strains, tensions, and, at times, feelings of guilt, of the more extreme mystics, subconscious eruptions necessarily occurred.

A person of normal, average abilities undergoing the pressures of the intensely ascetic, contemplative life, could easily fall prey to hallucinatory phantasmagoria which has been symbolized over the centuries by the Temptations of St. Anthony.

With the mystic, on the other hand, possessing innate abilities and living the highly concentrative life of the religious, it can almost be expected that a certain degree of poltergeist activity will be released. Other paranormal effects are also manifested, and Fr. Herbert Thurston's *The Physical Phenomena of Mysticism* provides a valuable study. Montague Summers also dealt with the subject in his work, *The Physical Phenomena of Mysticism*. However, this writing is characterized by a lack of critical discrimination and is written in an extremely credulous vein.

Parallel characteristics are very noticeable with the mystic and the medium. The production of physical paranormal effects are found with both, as well as telepathic and clairvoyant abilities. Telekinetic phenomena, luminous effects, teleplasm, and various sound manifestations have all been observed with the saints and mystics, as well as the mediums, and poltergeist phenomena has been recorded with both saints and mediums.

The one great difference between medium and mystic is easily recognized and consists primarily of ethical content. The saint and mystic are devoted to complete spirituality and the good of the human race, and their ethical natures when compared to the average person can only be described as superhumanly developed and advanced. As a result, excluding occasional poltergeist intrusions, their paranormal phenomena displays an equal ethical height.

The medium may be a very good person, but never approaches the spiritual peaks of the saint. On the other hand, the medium may fall prey to greed, and possessing a weak and highly suggestible nature, slip easily into deceit and dishonesty. In certain cases, mediums have been extremely unethical and truly despicable, and have been in many ways thoroughly undesirable individuals. Naturally, I am only speaking of those who have genuine paranormal abilities.

In direct parallel with western mystical axioms, the yogis of India, for example, teach that without proper purification of character, certain practices cannot be accomplished without unpleasant effects resulting from the release of the dregs of the subconscious with possible fearful hallucinatory and psychical effects. The Hindu theories of the paranormal nervous system, the chakras, etc., have certain similarities with the teachings of western mysticism and offer a number of interesting comparisons.

The Haunting of St. Vianney

Perhaps the best known example of haunting and poltergeist activity to have plagued a saint was that which occurred to St. John Baptist Vianney. St. Vianney is noted for other paranormal manifestations and it should come as no surprise to find that he became the victim of a violent poltergeist molestation that lasted for many years.

The poltergeist-haunting of St. Vianney probably began during the winter of 1824-1825, when the saint was beset by illness, both physical and psychological. His depression was characterized by feelings of divine rejection and a conviction of oncoming death. This period does seem to have been a depressive type that is very typical of many religious mystics just prior to what may be called the beginnings of their illumination and ecstatic experiences. In his case, however, the depression seems to have been exaggerated and partially of a morbid nature. At any rate, the poltergeist must have become active during this time.

As with the mystic, Teresa Higginson, the beginnings

of the haunting was characterized by poundings and rappings, and the curtains of his bed were disturbed. St. Vianney at first assumed that rats were about and when he attempted to repel them the manifestations typically became more violent.

The nature of the ghostly infestation soon became very violent and extremely complex. Voices were heard in a yard, but upon investigation could not be attributed to normal causes. At first reading, one may be tempted to suspect that such vocal effects were purely subjective and originated within the saint's mind. Perhaps during this haunting certain manifestations actually had no basis in reality, but it must be remembered that many happenings were witnessed by others.

For example, a nun heard a mysterious conversation that sounded as though an angry argument was taking place, and these voices were heard just as St. Vianney drew near.

The saint related a very strange, almost incredible experience during which he again heard voices in a yard. He likened the sounds to those created by a large assemblage of men, but noted that the voices were unintelligible, and sounded as though an unfamiliar language was spoken.

This curious incident, perhaps, has some obscure relationship to the phenomenon, "speaking in tongues." It has been observed that even though words spoken were reported by hearers to belong to languages familiar to them, nevertheless the actual "speech" was in reality an unintelligible, pseudo-language. In other words the "ability" of the hearer to "understand" such mysterious speech results from a purely subjective phenomenon having no basis in physical fact.

Interestingly, an Abbé who had assisted St. Vianney for eight years and another Abbé who had been with him for six years heard no abnormal sounds whatsoever. There are several possible reasons for this fact other than the obvious explanation that all reported noises were imaginary. One possibility—a very genuine possibility—is that some people are simply bad "receivers." There have been, it must be remembered, many examples of poltergeist-haunted houses wherein some occupants heard very loud, real sounds, yet others simply could not hear them.

Lest it be thought that all happenings described by the saint were unreal, certain incidents encountered by others as well as by St. Vianney will be described.

A wheelwright witnessed numerous mysterious events and offered his deposition to that effect. While staying with the saint he heard strange, loud noises within the presbytery, and on another occasion heard the door to his room shaken violently and simultaneously powerful, resounding blows struck the door.

As is so typical with the poltergeist, hatred of all matters religious was openly displayed. A witness told how he had seen a painting of the Annunciation spattered with filth and the picture was frequently defiled in this manner. It should be noted, regarding the poltergeists' ill-will aimed at things of a spiritual nature that St. Vianney was a noted exorcist and aided those who had experienced the fearful ordeals of traditional demonic possession.

The sister of the saint spent several nights in the haunted presbytery, and told how, during one night, she had heard violent, eerie poundings in the vicinity of her bed. The sounds ceased when she managed to light a lamp, but resumed in full force as soon as she attempted to return to sleep. She became so frightened that she left the infested building.

A particularly grotesque manifestation was reported by the saint when he related that the unseen intruder made strange, blowing noises and then apparently vomited on the floor. The ejected matter was described as appearing to have been some type of grain. With this incident, it is reasonable to suspect that a degree of subjective interpretation by the afflicted saint may have occurred. However, with the poltergeist, one simply cannot hold to any preconceived notions that limit one's belief regarding what is or is not possible. The world of psychism can be realistically compared to a phantasmagoria of incredible, unearthly manifestations quite unconcerned with personal theories and beliefs. I have, for example, encountered effects so bizarre and unbelievable that I would never commit them to print, and I confess that they are very seldom described.

One very famous incident involved a voice which was preceded by weird cries and a flurry of violent poundings on a door. The voice called the saint an eater of potatoes and threatened him.

Other times he experienced the eerie feeling of a ghostly hand touching his face and other not-so-pleasant personal attentions were given him.

A plasterer who had been commissioned to make a number of statues for St. Vianney said that he could not see how anyone could sleep in the haunted presbytery. He had stayed with the saint for a few nights and had heard mysterious and unexplained noises.

A policeman, near the traditional hour of midnight, heard an unexplainable, shocking shout, and other witnesses, of course, encountered the weird and unwanted manifestations of the poltergeist.

Strangely, no phenomena were reported by two young men who stayed with St. Vianney for twelve days other than one minor sound.

From the year 1845 the intensity of the phenomena gradually subsided and it is said that the long-suffering saint was seldom disturbed again by the poltergeist.

Other mystics have encountered spectral persecutions of perhaps equal violence and malignance, but the length of time that St. Vianney endured the haunting was remarkable.

It has been observed that the poltergeist does have a dual nature. Even though the manifestations displayed may show a malicious side, still little physical harm results. Exceptions are known, however, and the anti-religious aspect does represent a dark, disruptive facet.

Again, it is interesting to note that St. Vianney was an exorcist of fame and was considered to have been greatly endowed in the function of exorcism.

More Accounts of Haunted Saints

This story may have been changed to fit more orthodox views of devilish intervention, but at any rate it is of some interest.

While the saint lay in a sleepless rest he perceived a large, black dog which he recognized as of hellish origin. It was said to have been of enormous size, and to have possessed two horrible eyes. This fearful apparition rushed at the saint three times, but was defeated each time by the sign of the cross.

The appearance of the spectral dog is found in many stories, including the famous black poodle that confronted Faust in his study, and is very like the appearance of strange animals that were encountered during a number of the well-documented poltergeist cases. The animal-familiars of the witches are also brought to mind.

The probability that many of the stories telling of diabolic attacks upon the early saints were based upon actual fact is, to my mind, very strong. Naturally, the only available theory was that of demonic intervention, and any tales of mysterious manifestations were sure to have been altered to fit the devil concept. As a result, many of the legends of such persecutions must have been based upon examples of poltergeist attack, but at this late date it is near impossible to distinguish the real from the false.

I believe that St. Teresa of Avila may have run afoul of the poltergeist at times during her life, but the problem is complicated when it is remembered that she constantly mentioned that she saw devils, and in fact, visions of many types. Certain visions referred to problems and conditions that faced her during everyday life, and were often cast in symbolic form. There is little doubt that these experiences were of a subjective nature. One of the visions, for example, was of a hideous dwarf that gnashed his teeth and was described as a devil.

On one occasion when the saint was in choir she felt an urge of recollection and went out so that she would not disturb the other sisters. She wrote that those near her heard sounds of "great blows," and she heard voices that seemed to have been talking, but was unable to distinguish words. This incident is reminiscent of the voices that St. Vianney heard which he likened to those of an army speaking in an unknown language.

From *The Golden Legend* we read that St. Martin, while visiting a certain village, had a bed of straw made for him, but in the night left it to sleep on the ground. During the night the straw burst into flames and set his clothing on fire. According to the story he routed the flames by making the sign of the cross.

Naturally, this and similar stories from *The Golden Legend* are only valuable insofar as they show that tales of the poltergeist have undoubtedly come down through the centuries, even though in distorted and exaggerated form. The incident does suggest the fiery phenomena frequently found in cases where supernormal phenomena were present.

Certain incidents in the Life of St. Benedict are very suggestive of paranormal origin. It was reported that various monks occasionally heard voices, and they were interpreted as the devil quarreling with the saint. The devil opened the dialogue by calling St. Benedict's name twice, and annoyed at the lack of reply, asked why he was not accursed. The similarity of the "devil's" remarks to the voice that called St. Vianney by name, called him a "potato eater," and threatened to "get him" is very noticeable, and is thoroughly suggestive of poltergeist activity.

A description of another incident told how Satan, jealous of the austere reflection of St. Benedict, threw a rock at a little bell and broke it. Here we have an event that strikes much closer to home in that our old friend, the rock-tossing poltergeist, seems to have been busy. A parallel action was the molestation of the heritage of St. Godric by stone-throwings and other annoyances.

A story, which had clearly suffered alterations and exaggerations, told how St. Benedict miraculously extinguished a mysterious fire in a monastery kitchen. The flames didn't damage anything and did not behave in the manner of normal, earthly flames. In spite of the apparently exaggerated nature of the tale, there may be a kernel of truth in the story. It is possible that the legend actually sprang from an incident involving a fire of poltergeist origin, and as the years went by the story gradually underwent pious exaggerations and alterations. Unfortunately, the natural tendency to transform facts to fit beliefs is extremely strong and almost irresistible.

Such tales have no value as evidence whatsoever, but are still worthy of notice and study. As mentioned, they may have sprung from actual events during which real poltergeist phenomena occurred. We can easily see after investigating the lives of the more modern mystics and saints that paranormal phenomena present during their lives, including the unwelcome attentions of the poltergeist, could have also taken place with their predecessors. A complete study of the lives of the saints would turn up many stories of such a nature, I am sure.

During the life of St. Gemma Galgani, the stigmatist, a number of incidents occurred which suggest the intrusion of paranormal forces. She told how, on occasions, she was struck by blows from an invisible source, and reported an apparition of a phantasmic dog of diabolic nature. She was also said to have been thrown to the floor by the devil, and believed that the mysterious blows that struck her were caused by the demon.

Speculation in her case is greatly complicated by the fact that she gave all indications of an extremely neurotic nature and exhibited hysterical behavior. She continually saw visions of demons and angels, all acting according to the dictates of orthodox theology, and as a result it is difficult, if not impossible, to separate subjective experiences from objective phenomena. Unfortunately, those who were present during her presumed paranormal experiences were totally unaware, apparently, of hysterical symptoms and behavior.

The incident of being thrown to the floor by the devil can easily be explained by the well-known self-inflicted actions of hysterics. She could well have struck herself, and thrown herself about while undergoing hysterical seizures, and in all honesty believed that she had been persecuted by an outside agency. This possibility is reinforced by the fact that she continually expressed the desire to suffer and undergo complete abasement. With a highly emotional and unstable personality such as she seemed to have possessed, it is not difficult to assume that she did inflict upon herself unconsciously the various physical attacks that were reported. The possibility exists that actual poltergeist phenomena were witnessed in her presence, but it seems impossible to separate objective from subjective experiences in her case.

Another stigmatist, the Abbess la Madre Costante Maria, underwent somewhat similar experiences, and also manifested numerous hysterical manifestations.

There is, however, reason to suspect that occasionally genuine poltergeist phenomena were present with her.

The mystic, Teresa Higginson, encountered strange and violent manifestations which had all the "classical" features of the poltergeist. Weird shouts and loud poundings were reported in her presence, which, as could be expected, were attributed to the devil, and she was struck on the face on one occasion.

The hut of St. Abraham and surroundings were frequently disturbed and his matting was set ablaze periodically, according to stories of his life. It was said the cell of St. Pacomius was violently assailed by demonic manifestations, and, of course, the travails of St. Anthony are traditional. Included with other fantastic effects in his presence were the sounds of horses and breaking weapons. Again, tales such as these cannot have any value as evidence, due to the lack of critical documentation, but in spite of these limitations, the incidents may well have been real and of poltergeist origin.

There is no doubt whatsoever that a thorough study of the lives of the saints and mystics would uncover many more examples of obvious poltergeist phenomena, and a great many other cases that are highly suggestive of such paranormal activity.

CHAPTER HIGHLIGHTS

Religious mystics were prone to hauntings. The haunting of St. Vianney is an epic in poltergeist fury. A study of the lives of the saints would reveal many examples of hauntings that appear to be obvious poltergeist phenomena. History tends to show the saints were heavily involved in paranormal phenomena.

chapter 21

Conclusions—and Possible Explanations
of Poltergeist Phenomena

Possible Theories of Paranormal Activities

In our attempt to understand and perhaps explain to some degree the poltergeist—and hauntings—some order must be brought to the vast amount of material that is available for study. One limitation that we need have absolutely no worry about is any lack of subject matter!

Unfortunately, fraud has always entered into the picture and probably more so now than ever. It seems that the poltergeist has at last become popular! A number of cases over the years have proven to be the product of fraud. In fact the problem is undoubtedly increasing in scope for the simple reason that information concerning hauntings and poltergeists have become more available.

Previously, outside of a strictly limited number of people who were acquainted to some degree with the pursuit of psychical research and familiar with the scientific journals which now and then published accounts of hauntings, the poltergeist was little known. The spiritualists, of course, were familiar with such cases even though their concepts of the phenomena were overly simplified. With the above exceptions little information was publicly known, and that which has been circulated was considered by the educated to be superstitious folk-lore and foolish ghost stories. Little serious attention was paid to poltergeist reports. As we know, at a still earlier period, the answer was simply, witchcraft.

Today, however, the picture has changed drastically. Accounts of poltergeist cases are frequently described in newspaper articles—and in fact, every large newspaper has its ghostfile. Magazines exist devoted to accounts of oddities of all kinds ranging from flying saucers to phantoms, and they periodically carry stories of hauntings and poltergeists.

As a result of growing information, false and otherwise, the poltergeist has to some extent become a popular public figure. It could be easy for those desiring publicity and attention to acquire a bit of ephemeral fame by claiming that they are the object of a haunting.

In spite of the number of cases which have been invented, or improved upon, a great number are absolutely real. The problem is really little different than the investigation of mediumistic phenomena. First, we must eliminate fraud and mal-observation, and then the serious study can begin.

Perhaps the next problem to be met is the separation of certain phenomena which may or may not be the result of paranormal forces. After these "controversial" effects are placed in their right settings, the main study of the nature and origin of poltergeist and haunting manifestations can be undertaken.

The various theories advanced over the years attempting to explain poltergeist and haunting phenomena are briefly presented, and by comparing them with additional information. a certain amount of light can be shed upon a mysterious and fascinating subject.

An Early Advanced View

Paracelsus, for example, advanced an explanation for hauntings and poltergeists which is much like the view held by many spiritualists. He wrote in *De Animabus Mortuorum* that human spirits may appear as ghostly figures, or may stay unseen, calling attention to themselves by moving objects, knocking, throwing stones, groaning, walking, or whistling. It can be seen from this fragment that he was clearly aware of poltergeist phenomena, and the short list of effects that he gave include a good number of the characteristic attributes of the haunt. His view was actually far advanced for his time for he did not blame all unusual effects upon the workings of witchcraft, or the devil.

Views of Spiritualists

As I have mentioned, the average spiritualist of the present holds exactly the same view as above. I have been told by spiritualists that the ghostly manifestations of the poltergeist are simply due to a human spirit racing about throwing stones, setting fires, or moving objects all in the spirit of good, cheery "horseplay." When the apparent senselessness of certain of the effects is brought to mind then it is usually admitted that the erring and frenetic spirit was a bit on the childish side.

A variation of this thought is the substitution of "elementals" for human spirits. We have progressed no further. It is difficult enough to establish the existence of psychical phenomena, much less purely theoretical creatures whose being is utterly unsupported by any reliable evidence.

The "Theory" of Witchcraft

Of course, witchcraft was an all-inclusive answer, and its companion effect, diabolic possession, served in many cases.

The grotesque and evil side of the poltergeist fortified these theories, and in the absence of other information, provided logical and descriptive explanations. Much valuable material is given in modern and comparatively modern cases of possession, and such accounts are worthy of serious study.

The "Subconscious" Theory

The belief of the early spiritualists that all automatic communications by means of the planchette, ouija board, and automatic writing were of spirit origin, was dealt a hard blow when discoveries were made proving the existence of subconscious activity, secondary personality, and phenomena of dissociation. Soon, this knowledge was applied to spiritualistic phenomena, and step by step many manifestations thought to have been due to spirit intervention were demonstrated to have actually originated in various subconscious activities within a person.

In spite of the fact that informed spiritualists accepted and incorporated this knowledge of the subconscious into their philosophy, the majority of present day followers of spiritualism still accept without question the older belief of spirit activity.

The Theories of Various Scientists

The classic and widely known *From India to the Planet Mars* by Prof. Theodore Flournoy offers a marvelous example of the development of spiritoid personalities, pseudo-languages, memories of past incarnations, and the like, all of very normal origin. The phenomena presented is typical of the great majority of mediumistic effects that are not fraudulent, and the analysis that Prof. Flournoy made can be applied to such.

Sir William Barrett was particularly interested in poltergeist phenomena and had personally witnessed one example in action, as we know. He theorized that the child-medium usually involved in such cases was the equivalent of a solid particle of matter, which, when it falls into a saturated salt solution, produces a disturbance that results in the entire solution becoming a mass of crystals. He likened the poltergeist-medium to a nucleus representing the determining factor in the manifestations. He also insisted that it was quite possible for outside intelligence to aid in creating the effects, and with this suggestion the spiritistic theory was included.

Prof. Cesare Lombroso was frankly a spiritualist and it was his opinion that poltergeist and haunting manifestations were, in part, caused by the intervention of the dead. He also considered that on rare occasions hauntings were actually caused by a living person unconsciously "astrally" projected, inadvertantly creating ghostly phenomena. Certain apparitions are easily explained by this addition to the theory of bilocation. Prof. Lombroso's opinion is doubly valuable, for not only was he an experienced researcher, but he had personally observed a poltergeist disturbance on November 21, 1900, in Italy.

Prof. Camille Flammarion in his book *Haunted Houses,* arrived at much the same conclusion as did Prof. Lombroso. He admitted that a certain percentage of hauntings and poltergeist phenomena were unconsciously "committed" by women and hysterical girls by means of paranormal externalization of their "nerve energy." However he was also of the opinion that other effects were the products of spirits, and remarked that it would have been impossible to account for certain facts related in his book unless it was assumed that the spirits of the dead were directly involved.

Dr. Charles Richet stated that in his estimation there are two forms of hauntings. One type is the traditional haunted house, and the other is the haunted person. The last is what we would call a poltergeist-medium. As to the primary cause he preferred to remain undecided. However, inasmuch as he strongly opposed the spiritualistic as an explanation for mediumistic phenomena, he undoubtedly did not admit that it played any part in hauntings.

In his book *Poltergeist Over England,* Harry Price headed the last chapter, "Can We Explain the Poltergeist?" The very first word of that chapter was "No." He went on to say that there is definitely some relationship between poltergeists and puberty, and that the sexual functions are an important part of the phenomena. The fact that evidence indicates that poltergeists prefer little girls to boys is mentioned, and Price estimated that the ratio is roughly 95% to 5%. He admits that though this proportion is a fact, it cannot be explained at the present time.

Price also postulated a theory that a house, or a place, can store up an occult energy much as a battery, and can become saturated with the mental energy of a person in a state of emotional tension. He then said that such energy could remain in the haunted house, and under certain circumstance cause phantoms, or ghosts, to be seen or heard. Price also remarked, in reference to the spiritistic theory, that today no one really accepts the idea that poltergeists are spirits of the dead.

The hypothesis has been advanced that such paranormal manifestations are not merely chance effects, but are purposeful, and as certain psychological phenomena, are aimed at curative effects and the resolution of tensions and psychological conflicts. This opinion was given in a paper, *Psi Phenomena and Poltergeists* by Dr. John Layard, included in the *Proceedings*, Society for Psychical Research, July, 1944.

A similar psychoanalytic approach to the problem of the poltergeist has been urged by others, including Nandor Fodor. In the book *Haunted People*, Fodor's views were summed up in a sentence which said that the poltergeist can be explained by considering it a grouping of materialized and projected repressions. Fodor's opinion is nearly identical to the views expressed by Dr. Layard.

The author Sacheverell Sitwell, in his *Poltergeists, Fact or Fancy*, apparently does not believe that the major phenomena reported in so many cases existed, and prefers to think that the effects were due to faulty observations, and hysteria, and that this infection occasionally spread to other members of afflicted households. I doubt if anyone less biased than Sitwell would seriously contend that Prof. Lombroso, Sir William Barrett, Sir Oliver Lodge, Hereward Carrington, and others were given to mal-observation and hysteria. Sitwell did, I think, believe that paranormal rappings might be real.

Fr. Herbert Thurston accepted the reality of the reported phenomena and it has been said that he settled upon the point that, in some examples, diabolic intervention was excluded. He was also said not to have cared for the theory that a paranormal double projected by the process of bilocation, or ESP projection, was responsible for the ghostly disturbances so often witnessed. In his book, *Ghosts and Poltergeists*, he refused to speculate as to the ultimate cause of the phenomena.

Andrew Lang wrote that psychical science is forced to fall back upon the old belief that an actual spiritual being, a ghost, is present and active during haunting cases. He further remarked that we must finally admit that the beliefs considered to be savage and superstitious are correct after all, once it is admitted that a material, or semi-material, space-occupying ghost actually exists.

René Sudre believes that hauntings and poltergeist phenomena are entirely the creation of paranormal, subconscious actions. Spiritualistic theory has no place in his picture, and he ignores all evidence for ESP projection.

Theories for the appearance of phantasmic figures, or ghosts, have been advanced that cover a wide range of possibilities. G. N. M. Tyrrell suggests that phantoms are not actual space-filling beings in themselves, but are of psychological origin. An apparition, therefore, is a picture or an idea broadcast telepathically and when received is interpreted as a visual ghost. More simply stated, it is a telepathically induced hallucination. This opinion is given in his *Apparitions,* but does not explain the ghostly figures that have been seen, heard, and felt, singly and collectively, in many well-documented cases.

These are but a few of the opinions of researchers who have studied poltergeists and hauntings, but they account for the representative group of suggestions that have been and are being advanced today.

A Generally Popular Theory

A popular theory today is similar to that stated in Sudre's *Parapsychology* and it should be remembered that those who hold to this belief accept the reality of the major physical phenomena that have been reported.

Sudre first divides the phenomena into two main classes. One is false haunts, or poltergeist manifestations, which include movements of furniture and objects, thrown stones, rappings, ringing of bells, and the entire collection of phenomena that have been encountered with the poltergeist.

The other main class is hauntings and consists of very similar phenomena to that of the poltergeist, and includes the classic ghost. The phenomena, according to this theory, are more benign than that found with the poltergeist which in general can be said to be malicious. Sudre remarked that the phantoms found in hauntings do not require a medium and frequently are connected with a tragedy, as usually represented by tradition.

He states that the mechanism of the actual physical effects is teleplasmic in nature. It is not a form of telepathic action; but is due to a mediumistic subject influenced by local legend, and the like. The mediumistic subject may be at the site of the haunting, or may be far away. The phantoms are, therefore, created mentally. They are ideoplastic in form and represent the medium's thoughts. The same teleplasmic origin for poltergeist manifestations is also assumed, and the presence of a mediumistic subject is postulated.

Sudre further states that suggestion, local traditions, and psychological activities including resentments, repressions, and conflicts are motivating forces behind both classes of phenomena.

This general theory is over-inclusive and attempts to explain away much of the phenomena found in hauntings and with the poltergeist. However, there are other effects that do not fall into line so easily. In fact, by such reasoning I would be hard put to prove my own independent existence.

I am inclined, more or less, to merge poltergeist phenomena and hauntings into one general group, and find it very difficult and arbitrary to sharply split them into divisions. Identical phenomena are found in both classes. Ghostly appearances, movements of objects, poundings, and sounds of all descriptions are commonly found with each class of phenomena.

Some are inclined to believe that poltergeist phenomena are less patterned and less intelligent than hauntings. Hauntings are considered to be more "spiritoid in nature," and give the appearance of being caused by actual, independent spirits of the dead. Whether or not these apparent spirits are true entities, or merely projections of the subject's—the medium's—mind as Sudre and other researchers suspect, is another problem.

Nevertheless, during known, obvious poltergeist cases, phantoms have been seen and heard that gave every indication of having been spirits of the dead. On occasion, phantoms have indicated that they were spirits of dead relatives of witnesses present.

Resolving the Main Problem

It seems, then, that the main problem is not the reality or non-reality of such phenomena, but rather the nature of the motivating force behind it. The evidence for the actual existence of these paranormal effects is overwhelming. We have report after report of excellent quality describing cases of all kinds. Evidence is supported by a still larger amount of proof which is not as well-documented but nevertheless offers a vast quantity of supplementary, valuable material. In truth, the evidence for the reality of the poltergeist and hauntings is so enormous that I cannot see how it can be judged as anything but conclusive.

For myself, I have had the good fortune to have witnessed several examples of poltergeist and haunting phenomena, and have also had the opportunity to study other cases closely. As a result of these experiences I cannot help but place credence in the reports of others who have investigated competently and thoroughly. Consequently, the acceptance of such phenomena offers not too great a mental hurdle, but this acceptance is only applied to individual cases and does not imply a blanket belief. Each case must be judged on its own merits.

The mechanistic theory mentioned is entirely too inclusive, and can easily be used to explain too much. When a theory becomes so all-inclusive, it is more an article of faith than a scientific convenience. It becomes a tool to discredit another theory and as such is enlarged beyond its legitimate boundaries. Those who accept survival of bodily death as a working theory are in a far less limited position, for they encompass the mechanics of the materialistic theories as well as the concept of survival. It may seem strange to apply the term materialist to those engaged in the study of psychical science, but strictly speaking, that is exactly what they are. It can be correctly said that they are materialists who accept certain paranormal phenomena as fact, or at least as possible fact.

Astral Projection

The phenomena of bilocation, or ESP projection, (astral projection) has crucial bearing upon any explanation of poltergeist phenomena. Its application to hauntings is obvious. If its reality is admitted then survival and the spiritistic origin for a percentage of such manifestations becomes obvious.

Naturally the subject of ESP projection cannot be dealt with here except to briefly mention the subject and its application to poltergeist phenomena and hauntings. The term ESP projection, as is well known, simply means the separation of the consciousness—or "soul"—from the body either spontaneously or at will, and this separated consciousness is at times capable of travel under control or partial control of the will.

Prof. Hornel Hart has presented material of the utmost importance regarding his subject and his writings should be consulted.[1]

Dr. Robert Crookall has compiled extensive evidence in his *Study and Practice of Astral Projection, The Techniques of Astral Projection, More Astral Projection,* and other works, and remarked appropriately in a preface that the evidence for the existence of such phenomena is of such amount that it equals that which establishes the theory of evolution.

Sylvan Muldoon's *Projection of the Astral Body and The Phenomena of Astral Projection,* and Suzy Smith's *The Enigma of Out-of-Body Travel* are of great value.

There is, naturally, much more evidence including that to be found in publications of the Society for Psychical Research, and similar publications. In fact, many books deal with the subject, some of worth and others written from a non-scientific viewpoint. The evidence for the existence of ESP projection is truly great in extent and cannot be ignored.

Sylvan Muldoon wrote in his *Projection of the Astral Body* that he found it impossible to influence material objects while projected, with two exceptions. His first experience wherein he was able to affect an object occurred during a severe attack of stomach pains when he attempted to get out of bed and reach a door so that he could call for help. He was unable to do so and fainted. Muldoon relates that he awoke from this faint, "projected," and went to his mother's bedside. A gap took place in his consciousness, and upon regaining awareness, he observed his mother and small brother

[1]*The Enigma of Survival.*

ESP Projection: Spontaneous cases and the experimental method, Journal ASPR 48, (1954).

Six Theories About Apparitions: A co-operative report with associated collaborators in the International Project for Research on ESP Projection, Proceedings, SPR 50 (1956).

in a state of confusion talking excitedly about their mattress having pitched them out of bed.

At this point Muldoon was swept back into his own room and reuinted with his normal, physical body. He called out to his mother, and she came and told him how she had been thrown from her bed by the mattress.

The second experience Muldoon describes tells how during a dream he pounded upon a very large oil-tank by his house. The noise of the blows startled him, and he remembered returning to awaken in his physical body. He stated that he heard the blows still resounding from the metal tank while fully conscious, and mentioned that other witnesses testified that they had also heard the pounding upon the tank.

According to Muldoon's description, phenomena exactly paralleling some poltergeist manifestations were produced by his projected "astral" form. As you can easily see, the relationship of projection and poltergeist is clearly indicated by these two incidents.

A Final Outlook to Consider

I find it not too difficult to blend the many theories into one inclusive explanation. Each theory that has been briefly mentioned has been the result of observation and experimentation, and must as such represent at least one part of the total picture. Therefore, if all are taken into consideration, and the best elements taken from each, a far more workable concept of the poltergeist must result.

This theory can be briefly stated: Psychical phenomena in many of its manifestations can be considered the product of paranormal energies and "ectoplasmic" material exuded from a mediumistic subject. This plasm is shaped into phantasmic forms of all kinds, and is also responsible for various telergic, or telekinetic, effects such as the movements of objects and throwing of rocks. Other manifestations including temperature changes, spontaneous fires and the like may result from other mechanisms. The plasmic material available is ideoplastic, and is molded into the many varied forms that have been seen. The resultant phenomena can be the product of subconscious activities.

A certain percentage of poltergeist and haunting phenomena can also be instigated by spirits of the dead who are capable of utilizing the mechanism mentioned. Extremely complex cases and cases that include phantoms that speak, and give all indications of intelligence and awareness, may fall into this category. Others may well be of spiritistic origin, but are of a nature that makes classification difficult, and at times, impossible.

Cases also must exist which blend spiritistic and subconscious origins together. The case entitled "An Indian Poltergeist" included in Fr. Thurston's collection fits perfectly into this category.

Price's concept, which is really a variation of the well-known theory of psychometry, stating that a house may absorb psychical emanations and release them in the presence of mediumistic subjects, is also included in our theory.

In general, it can be said that the nature of the poltergeist-force is mostly unpleasant and on occasion vicious. This has been a problem that has caused considerable concern, but can be solved by remembering that the nature of many subconscious activities is of a malicious order. During a typical poltergeist case psychological tensions and repressions are liberated which can result in paranormal effects mirroring these unpleasant mental states.

Cases of spiritistic origin, which show this evil nature can be a blend of two things. One is that an infesting spirit can be simply—evil. The other is that a case can offer phenomena influenced by subconscious activities which are of an unpleasant type, and still simultaneously present benign, spirit-motivated effects.

CHAPTER HIGHLIGHTS

There is no lack of material from which to investigate the poltergeist. Fraud occasionally has entered into the picture but can be detected. In antiquity, witchcraft was an all-inclusive explanation of poltergeist. An extended discussion of the theories of various scientists, researchers and spiritualists has been set out. A general popular theory of the present is similar to that of Sudre, but actually is inadequate. Bilocation or astral projection has crucial bearing upon theories of poltergeist origins. The most mature present outlook on poltergeist and hauntings is through a concept based on the best elements of each school of thought set out in the chapter. Inanimate objects can absorb physical energies and release phenomena in the presence of certain mediumistic persons.